Global Issues in Action:
Tasks that Work

Kozo YANAGAWA / Simon JOHNSON

SANSHUSHA

音声ダウンロード＆ストリーミングサービス（無料）のご案内

https://www.sanshusha.co.jp/onsei/isbn/9784384335057/

本書の音声データは、上記アドレスよりダウンロードおよびストリーミング再生ができます。ぜひご利用ください。

この本で教え，学ぶみなさんへ

　言葉を交わすという行為は，相手を受け入れ，相手に自分を開こうとする試みに他なりません。楽しかったことやうれしかったこと，つらかったことを共有し，お互いが前よりも少しだけわかり合うとすること―それが，人が言葉を交わすことの理由の一つなのかもしれません。

　この教科書は，言葉を交わすことの意味をこのように考えて作りました。それが言葉（英語）を学ぶ強い動機になると考えたからです。

　ですが，言葉を交わす，心を通わせることは，それだからこそ少し勇気がいることではないでしょうか。教師は高い教壇から降り，平場で生徒や学生に語りかけてみてはどうでしょうか。生徒や学生はクラスメートに身体と視線を向けるだけでも，自分をひらき，相手を受け入れる準備が整うでしょう。

　この教科書で，みなさんが英語という言葉を使って気持ちや考えを伝え合い，Global issue は自分自身の問題であったと気づいてもらえればうれしく思います。

著者

この本の使い方

この本の目標

1. Global issue を自分の問題として受けとめ，地球市民の一人としてその問題の解決を志向できる。
2. その実現のために，自分の想いを他者と英語で伝え合うことができる。

構成と内容の特徴

☐ Global issue を俯瞰する章（Chapters 1-5），詳しく調べる章（Chapters 6-10），そして行動する章（Chapters 11-15）の3部構成。

☐ 3章と4章，6章と7章，9章と10章は内容的につながっています。

☐ Chapter ごとに構成が異なります。次に何が来るかわからない怖さと楽しみがあります。

☐ Global issue だけでなく，個人的・日常的話題も取り上げます。両者は地続きであると考えるためです。

タスクの特徴

☐ **わくわくするタスク**：今の英語力で伝え合うことを優先します。使用する表現や語彙をことさらに示し，それらを機械的に練習することはあえてしません。

☐ **当事者として向き合うタスク**：この教科書のいたるところでみなさんに問いを投げかけています。みなさん自身に Global issue と向き合ってほしいからです。

☐ **順序立てられたタスク**：前のタスクが後のタスクの足場になるように配列してあります。それによって英語で表現することが前よりも少し自由になります。

☐ **一体感のあるタスク**：クラス全員で楽しめる Chapters を2つ収録しました。Chapter 8（Who are the *Barumbans*?），Chapter 15（*Another Story*）の2つです。どちらか1つでもチャレンジしてみてください。せっかくこの教科書に出会ったのですから。

☐ **選りすぐられたタスク**：著者の長年にわたる実践から，選りすぐられたタスクのみを収録しました。

タスクの4種類

Task	必須タスク。
Optional task	興味関心や必要に応じて実施。
Wrap-up	まとめ的タスク。
Language	タスクを遂行するのに役立つ表現を学びます。

タスクの効果を最大化するために，次のアイコンで示される 4 つの動作を覚えましょう。

- □ ジャンケン 🖐
- □ パートナーを変える
- □ パートナーを維持したまま役割を交代する
- □ 教科書を閉じる ・開く

パートナーの変え方：4 人をユニットとして，ペアの相手を変えます。

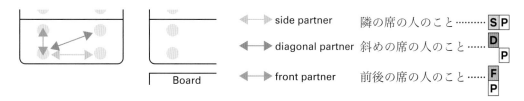

⟷ side partner	隣の席の人のこと…………	S P
⟷ diagonal partner	斜めの席の人のこと……	D P
⟷ front partner	前後の席の人のこと……	F P

※各章末の QR コードには，学生（生徒）の writing 提出用原稿やプレゼンテーション（Chap. 5）の評価票等が収録されています。

名札の利用のススメ ～授業をイキイキさせるために～

□ 作り方

- ●ネームフォルダを用意します。100 円ショップや生協で買えます。
- ●名札の両面に学籍（出席）番号と名前をフルネームで書きます。
- ●学籍（出席）番号や学科毎に異なった色で縁取りしてもよいでしょう。

□ 使い方

- ●授業開始前：クラスの誰かが，4 人を 1 グループとしてランダムに名札を座席に置きます（**パートナーの変え方**参照）。学生（生徒）は，自分の名札が置いてある座席に座ります。
- ●授業終了後：名札は回収します。学生（生徒）は先生が用意した入れ物（封筒やバッグ）に各自で戻します。回収した名札で，先生が出席確認をする場合もあります。

Contents
目次

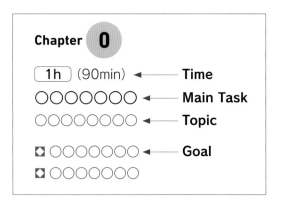

Step 1	Global issue を俯瞰する

1h

インフォメーションギャップ
日常的・個人的話題

◘ クラスの責任あるメンバーの一人として，クラス内に良好な人間関係を築くことができる。
◘ 適切な声量とアイコンタクトで，やりとりを維持・発展させることができる。

1h

語り・エッセイライティング
核問題

◘ 興味のある Global issue について, 写真を用いて 1 分間, 英語でまとまりのある話ができる。
◘ 興味のある Global issue について，100-150 語のエッセイを書くことができる。

1h

問題解決
ストレス・不安

◘ 自分の抱える不安や悩みを伝えることができる。
◘ 助言を与え，相手の行動を促すことができる。

Step 3 Global issue に行動する

Chapter 1

Introduction to global issues

 Can-dos
◎クラスの責任あるメンバーの一人として，クラス内で良好な人間関係を築くことができる。
◎適切な声量とアイコンタクトで，やり取りを維持・発展させることができる。

Task 1 　How positive are you about life?

1 Speak up

Your teacher will ask the class a few questions.

- Have you ever been abroad?
- Have you ever worked part-time?
- ...

2 Talk　SP (side partner)

Ask each other the following questions. Say more than just "Yes" or "No."

- Have you ever been abroad?
- Have you ever worked part-time?
- Have you ever seen a ghost?
- ...

Example

Keita : Have you ever been abroad, Fumi?

Fumi : Yes, I've been to Hawaii.

Keita : Did you go alone?

Fumi : No, I went with my family.

Keita : How was the trip?

Fumi : Awesome! We stayed on Hawaii Island instead of Oahu.

Keita : What did you like most about Hawaii Island?

Lava in Hawaii Island

Fumi : There was so much to love there! My favorite things were the starry night sky and the lava spilling into the Pacific Ocean from the active volcanoes.

Keita : I've been to Hawaii, too, but never Hawaii Island. Next time I'll definitely go there. Thanks, Fumi.

Fumi : You're welcome.

3 **Listen** Your teacher will explain the system for changing partners in this class.

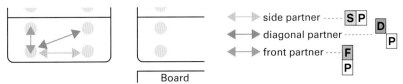

Board

4 **Talk** $\frac{F}{P}$ (front partner)

Ask each other the following questions.

- Have you ever cheated on an examination?
- Have you ever told a lie?
- Have you ever skipped a class?
- ...

(**Task 2**) **What do you have in common?**

1 **Talk and list** $\frac{D}{P}$ (diagonal partner)

① Take out a blank sheet of paper.

② Ask each other questions to find out what you have in common. Try to identify as many things you have in common as possible. Say more than just "Yes" or "No."

③ List the things you have in common and count them up. The partners with the most things in common are the class winners.

Things that you and your partner have in common
· 19 years old
· ...
· ...
Total number _____

Example

Yuta : I'm Yuta, from Yokohama. It's nice to meet you. Where are you from?

Sei : I'm Sei, also from Yokohama. I'm so proud of my city. It's nice to meet you, too.

Yuta : Do you work part-time? I teach math to junior high school students.

Sei : Good for you. I work part-time at a convenience store. Have you ever been abroad?

Yuta : I have been to Hawaii. It was fantastic. How about you?

Sei : I've also been to Hawaii, with my family. We had a wonderful time.

Yuta : What month were you born in?

Sei : In August. Maybe that's why I love summer activities like scuba diving and camping. How about you?

Yuta : ...

2 Go to the board

Who are the winners?

① Your teacher will jot down the numbers 20 to 1 (Board 1).

② Your teacher will ask each pair of partners to write their names next to the number of things they have in common.

③ Congratulate the winning partners.

```
20 Yuki & Taisei
19 Daiki & Harumi, Keita & Natsumi
18 Fumiyasu & Haruna
17 Saki & Miki
16
15
14 Ryo & Yoko, Miyu & Chinatsu
13
12 Mako & Sho, Tetsushi & Riku, Rui & Haruka
11
10
......
```

Board 1

Task 3 What are your partner's good points?

1 Listen

Your teacher will pick out a student and shower her with compliments.

Example

🔊
05

Teacher : You look so kind!

Chiharu : Do I?

Teacher : You also have a wonderful smile.

Chiharu : Thank you. I'm very happy to hear that.

Teacher : And your shirt looks great on you. I love the color and design.

Chiharu : Thank you again! I just bought this shirt at Uniqlo.

2 Talk Admire your partner

① Take 30 seconds to carefully examine your S P and think of as many good things about them as possible.

② Point out good things about your partner for 1 minute, and listen to your partner point out good things about you (🀄 to decide who goes first).

Optional task | **What are your good points? Write down the things your partner pointed out.**

List

- ...

- ...

- ...

Task 4 — Introduction to Global Issues

1 Speak up

① Your teacher will ask the class to think of some global issues and write them down on the board.

② Go to the board, add a global issue to the list, and write down your name. Everyone must contribute (Board 2).

③ Your teacher will ask why the issues listed on the board are important.

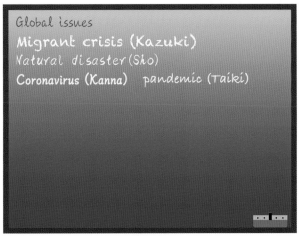

Board 2

2 Talk F / P

① Talk for one-minute about a global issue that interests you, and listen to your partner do the same (🔁 to decide who goes first).

② 🔄 .

◉ Homework for Chapter 2 (p.14)

Find a photograph about a global issue that interests you. The photo should be large (A4 size or larger), and preferably in color. Prepare to present a one-minute talk on the topic in the next class.

2 Show and tell

Can-dos
◉ 興味のある Global issue について，写真を用いて 1 分間，英語でまとまりのある話ができる。
◉ 興味のある Global issue について，100-150 語のエッセイを書くことができる。

Task 1 — Get your homework ready (see p.13) and talk about the global issue that interests you.

1 Talk

① 🙋 with your S P .

② **Winner**: Show your photo and begin your 1-minute talk.

   Loser: Make comments and ask questions.

③ ●⇄●

④ ⟨⟩

photo 1

2 Volunteer to present a talk to the class

Task 2 — Show and tell

1 Speak up

🔊
06

Your teacher will show the class a photo (photo 2) and ask a couple of questions. Answer the questions. Here are some examples:

• Have you ever heard of ICAN?

• Do you know what ICAN stands for?

photo 2   EPA=JiJi

2 Listen

Your teacher will offer an opinion about the ICAN protest pictured in photo 2 .

Example

A global issue: ICAN

🔊
07

This picture (photo 2) shows activists holding up an ICAN banner. ICAN stands for the International Campaign to Abolish Nuclear Weapons, a campaign to promote the Treaty on the Prohibition of Nuclear Weapons. The ICAN organizers were awarded the Nobel Peace Prize in 2017. Yet Japan and many other countries have not signed the treaty ICAN promotes. Why has Japan chosen not to sign? Japan is the only country to have suffered the horrific destructive force of the atomic bomb. As you know, the atomic bombs dropped on Hiroshima and Nagasaki by the US Air Force in 1945 killed up to 230,000 people. With such a history, Japan should take a leading role in abolishing nuclear weapons. I admit that Japan is protected by the nuclear umbrella provided by the US. Even so, Japan must take the initiative to organize and support international efforts to stop nuclear weapons. Thank you.

3 **Talk** Pair up with your DP and ask each other the questions below.

- Did you know that atomic bombs were dropped on Hiroshima and Nagasaki?
- How many people were killed by the atomic bombs?

4 1) **Speak up** Your teacher will ask the class a few questions (Board 1) about the photograph of the ICAN activists.

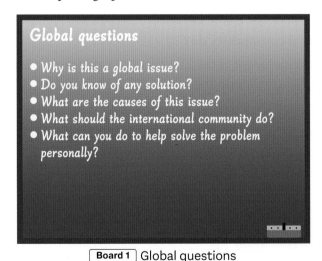

Global questions

- Why is this a global issue?
- Do you know of any solution?
- What are the causes of this issue?
- What should the international community do?
- What can you do to help solve the problem personally?

Board 1 Global questions

2) **Talk** Pair up with your SP and ask each other the questions (Board 1) about ICAN.

1 Read aloud and translate

① 🗣 with your ▣FP.

② Read your part (**Winner**: Tsubasa, **Loser**: Eri) aloud with your partner.

🔊 08

Tsubasa : **Why is this a global issue?**

Eri : Because nuclear weapons threaten the entire world with an extraordinary loss of human life.

Tsubasa : That's true. **What are the causes of this issue?**

Eri : Well, nuclear weapons have long been believed to be effective in preserving world peace as deterrents* against the use of conventional military forces.

Tsubasa : So removing nuclear weapons would remove a deterrent against war.

Eri : Another obstacle is the widespread use of nuclear resources for energy. Nuclear power is more stable and reliable than conventional sources such as water and wind, and more environmentally friendly than coal or natural gas. But the reactors in nuclear power plants can create materials used for nuclear weapons.

Tsubasa : **Do you know of any solution?**

Eri : I can't think of any immediate solutions, but I'm convinced we should never give up. Nuclear weapons threaten the whole planet.

Tsubasa : **What should the international community do?**

Eri : Well, all five of the permanent members of the UN Security Council possess nuclear weapons. Russia alone has more than six thousand nuclear warheads, and the US has almost as many. If they possess nuclear weapons themselves, we can hardly count on them to help solve the problem. Instead, we have to rely on non-governmental organizations such as ICAN to take action.

Tsubasa : **What can you do to help solve the problem personally?**

| Russia | USA | France | China | UK | Pakistan | India | Israel | North Korea |
| 6,500 | 6,185 | 300 | 290 | 200 | 150-160 | 130-140 | 80-90 | 20-30 |

Figure 1 Nuclear warheads

Eri : There's not much I can do as an individual, but I will continue to discuss the issue and observe new developments.

*deterrent = a thing that discourages someone from doing something

③ 🎧 Listen and repeat.

④ 🔄 and read the dialogue aloud again.

⑤ Translate your part aloud in Japanese.

2 Check your understanding Take turns asking the questions below.

- Why does Eri think nuclear energy is justified? List her arguments.
- Does Eri expect the UN Security Council to stop nuclear weapons?
- Does Eri think that she can help stop nuclear weapons as an individual?

3 Discuss the questions below

- Why do you think Japan hasn't signed the treaty, Treaty on the Prohibition of Nuclear Weapons?
- Do you think Japan should take a more active role in banning nuclear weapons?

Task 4   Back to your 1-minute talk about the photo

1 Talk

① 🗣 with your ^D_P.

Winner: Ask your partner the questions below.

Loser: Answer the questions.

- Why is this/that a global issue?
- Do you know of any solution?
- What should the international community do?
- What can you do to help solve the problem personally?

②

2 Stand up and talk Improve your speech

① Stand up together and 🗣 with your S P.

Winner: Begin your speech. Incorporate the answers to the global questions (Board 1)

Loser: Ask questions or make comments.

②

③ Sit down.

3 Write up Take 15 minutes to write out an improved version of your 1-minute talk. Turn in the version to the teacher.

A global issue that interests me

Optional task

Volunteer to present a talk to the class.

Help me!

Can-dos
◎自分の抱える不安や悩みを伝えることができる。
◎助言を与え，相手の行動を促すことができる。

Task 1) Help your teacher

1 Speak up

Your teacher will ask about your problems. Describe your problems to the rest of the class.

Example

11

A : What's troubling you these days?

B : I am so stressed out by my upcoming exams. [explaining a problem]

A : Are you? Why don't you do something to relax? [giving advice]

B : I tried, but ...

2 Listen

Your teacher has a personal problem to share with the class.

3 Talk

Pair up with your S P and take turns asking each other, "What would you do if you were in your teacher's shoes?"

Task 2) What's troubling you these days?

① **Describe** your problem and how you feel. Take 2 minutes to prepare a description of a problem in your life.

② 🗣 with your F/P .

Winner : Describe your problem and ask for help.

Loser : Listen and offer advice.

③ ●⇄●

④ ⬊⬈

Fill in the blanks

🔊 12

a) Jack was (emb   ) to be seen on the street in his pajamas.

b) Last week I ran into my ex-boyfriend on the subway. We had an (awk   )
   conversation.

c) The noisy children (ann   ) the other customers in the restaurant last
   night.

d) I'm (afr   ) that Miyu will be angry.

e) Honoka was (disc   ) by her test score. She decided to give up math.

f) The loss of my pet was a painful and (upse   ) experience.

g) Tom was never invited to his coworkers' parties. He felt (isol   ) and
   alone.

Fill in the blanks and role play

① Complete Table 1 .

② 🗣 with your D/P .

   Winner: Person with problems

   Loser: Advice-giver

③ Read the problems aloud and confirm them, one by one.

④ ●⇄●

🔊 13

Table 1   Confirm the problems

	Person with problems	Advice-giver
ex. 1	It takes me forever to get to sleep at night.	Does it?
ex. 2	I have a slight cold.	Do you?
a)	I'm getting fat these days.	( )( )?
b)	My friends are always pressuring me to become a vegetarian.	( )( )?
c)	I'm addicted to online gaming.	( )( )?
d)	I can't live without my smartphone.	( )( )?

Task 3 · What is your addiction?

☐ Talk

① Pair up with your S P and take turns asking each other, "What are you addicted to?"

② 🔄

Language / 3 / How soft are the suggestions?

1 Choose Which of the four suggestions below sound softer than the others?

🔊 14

a) Have you considered telling the police?
b) You should tell the police.
c) Tell the police.
d) You must tell the police.
e) You might want to tell the police.
f) Why don't you tell the police?
g) I suggest that you tell the police.
h) If I were you, I'd tell the police.
i) You need to tell the police.

2 Talk

🗣 with your F/P and take turns asking each other,

"What would you do if you found 10,000 yen on the street?"

Task 4 · What's troubling Risako?

① 🗣 with your D/P .

Winner: Risako
Loser: Misaki

② Read the dialog aloud. Maintain eye contact.

Risako : Yuri is stressing me out.

Misaki : **Is she?** What happened? I thought that you two were getting along fine.

Risako : We are getting along, but she comes over in the evening and stays for many hours. If she came occasionally, that would be okay. But recently she has been showing up two or three times a week. With more time to myself, I could relax with a book or get some studying done.

Misaki : I see. You **might want to** tell her how you really feel.

Risako : I'm afraid that would make her sad or upset.

Misaki : You worry too much. Just be honest and tell her that you need more time to yourself. Yuri will understand.

Risako : Thank you, Misaki. I'll try that.

③ 🎧 Listen and repeat.

④ [◐⇄◑] and read the dialog out loud again.

⑤ Talk Ask each other, "Have you ever had the same problem as Risako?"

         ○ If yes, share the experience with your partner.

         ○ If no, what would you do if you were in Risako's shoes?

(**Task 5**) **Share your problem**

Share your problem with your [F/P].

Optional task 1

Share your problem with the class and solve it!

(**Task 6**) **Help your partner**

① Fill in Complete the following sentences about personal problems.

share	fallen in love	break up with	gaining weight
bullying	what I can do	late for	to come

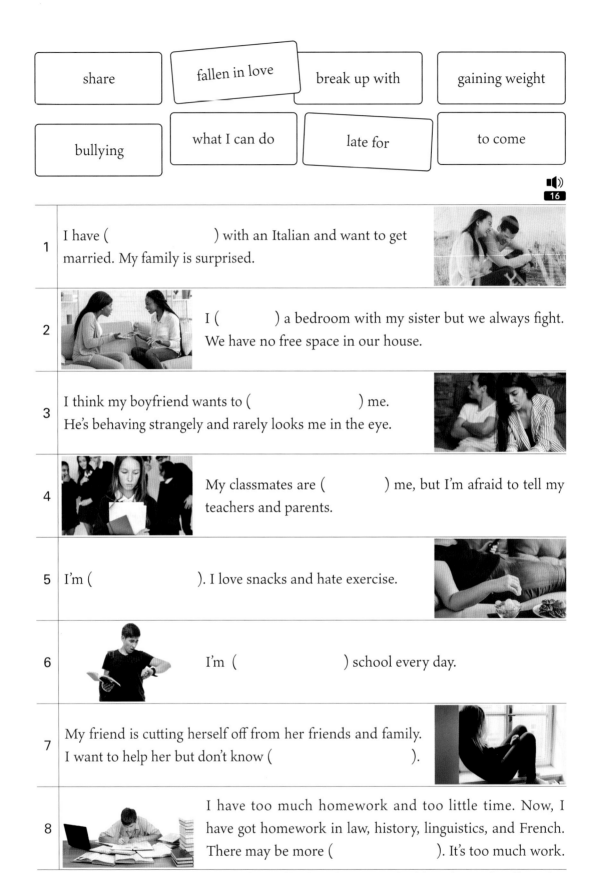

1. I have ( ) with an Italian and want to get married. My family is surprised.

2. I ( ) a bedroom with my sister but we always fight. We have no free space in our house.

3. I think my boyfriend wants to ( ) me. He's behaving strangely and rarely looks me in the eye.

4. My classmates are ( ) me, but I'm afraid to tell my teachers and parents.

5. I'm ( ). I love snacks and hate exercise.

6. I'm ( ) school every day.

7. My friend is cutting herself off from her friends and family. I want to help her but don't know ( ).

8. I have too much homework and too little time. Now, I have got homework in law, history, linguistics, and French. There may be more ( ). It's too much work.

② **Talk**

Pair up with your **F**/**P** and take turns asking for help, one by one (problems 1 to 8).

Wrap-up

Write out your personal problem. You have 15 minutes.

The world is waiting for your help

Can-dos
◉ Global issues を当事者の一人としてとらえ，考えることができる。
◉ 困難や不安を抱える人々に，助言を与えることができる。

Task 1 What's the problem?

1 Speak up

Your teacher will ask the class a few questions about
photo 1 .

🔊 17

- What do you see in the picture?
- Where do you think this is?
- What do you think they are doing?
- ...

photo 1

©UNICEF/UNI187489/Noorani
提供：（公財）日本ユニセフ協会

Task 2 Poverty

1 Read in silence

🔊 18

The most massive, immediate problem is poverty. A surprising number of people—more than a third of the world's population—are leading miserable lives as a result of poverty. Three-fifths of the 4.4 billion people living in developing countries lack basic sanitation. A third of them have no access to clean water. A quarter live in sub-standard housing. A fifth have no access to modern health services. Twenty percent are chronically

photo 2 Rio in Brazil

ill because they lack adequate nutrition. A fifth of the children in developing countries never make it to the end of primary school. Poverty is a crisis for all of humanity. It demands attention now.

2 Check your understanding

🔊 19

Pair up with your $\frac{F}{P}$ and take turns asking each other the questions below.

- What is the massive, immediate problem according to the text above?
- How many people in developing countries have no access to clean water?
- What basic resources and services are required for living?

3 | Speak up

Your teacher will ask the class a few questions about the text.

■)) 20

- What is basic sanitation?
- What are modern health services?
- ...

4 | Talk

Pair up with your [D][P] and take turns asking each other the question below.

- Have you ever lacked access to clean water, basic sanitation, or modern health services?
  - If yes, share the experience.
  - If no, how would you manage such a problem?

5 | Build your vocabulary

■)) 21

table 1

☑	English	Japanese
❏	massive, immediate problem	
❏	developing countries	
❏	4.4 billion people	
❏	modern health services	
❏	basic sanitation	
❏	have no access to clean water	
❏	demand attention	
❏	a third / one-third	
❏	a quarter / one-quarter	
❏	three-fifths	

1) Translate the terms above from English to Japanese.
2) Memorize
   ① with your [S][P] .

   Winner : Translate the first phrase above into Japanese and say it out loud.

   Loser : Close this book 📕 and translate the phrase back into English.

   ② Do the same for the other phrases, checking the boxes ☑ as you go.

   ③ ●⇄●

3) Respond

①

② Your teacher will read out the words and phrases in Japanese, one by one. Work with the rest of the class to translate the Japanese phrases back into English.

Optional task

Pair up with your **D** **P** and take turns asking each other the question,

"What is the most pressing problem in your life?"

Task 3 **Is poverty the only problem?**

1 **Describe and discuss**

🔊 22

Pair up with your **S** **P** and take turns asking each other the following questions about [photo 3] and [photo 4] .

- Do you think that the turtle has access to clean water?
- What would you say if you were the turtle?
- What is the massive, immediate problem?
- Who do you think is responsible for this?
- How do you think this problem affects humans?
- Can you do anything to help solve this problem?
- ...

[photo 3] ©Fotos593/Shutterstock.com

[photo 4] ©NULL/Alamy Stock Photo

2 **Make up a story** about [photo 3] **&** [photo 4].

1. Take 10 minutes to make up a story with three characters: a plastic bottle, a turtle, and a fisherman.
2. One of you will share the story with the class. Decide who.

Task 4 **Are poverty and sea pollution the world's only problems?**

1 **Fill in the blanks**

Complete the following sentences about personal problems. Use the words and phrases from the list.

tightened	detained	am depressed	strong accent

atomic bombings	fled	self-isolated

🔊 23

1	We ( ) to Lebanon from Syria, but our life here is harsh. We have no jobs, no money, and nothing to eat. The global community has deserted us. [22-year-old woman, Syria]	
2		English is my second language. I speak English well enough to work part-time as an assistant language teacher (ALT), but my students sometimes have trouble understanding my ( ). [23-year-old English teacher, France]
3	My parents were killed in the ( ) when I was ten. I went to live with my uncle in Fukuoka. I feel sad when I think back to those days. [84-year-old plumber, Japan].	
4		I ( ) to protect my family and co-workers from the virus. I would love to see them now. [21-year-old nurse, Italy].
5	My close friends were ( ) in North Korea. [59-year-old engineer, South Korea]	
6		In spite of my wonderful family and successful career, I ( ) these days. [35-year-old movie star, Greece]
7	I want to emigrate to the US to escape my hard life in Mexico, but the US government has ( ) immigration controls. [28-year-old construction worker, Mexico]	

(1)©Nuki Sharir/Shutterstock.com (2)©Krakenimages.com/Shutterstock.com (3)©curraheeshutter/Shutterstock.com (4)©Liudmyla Guniavaia/Shutterstock.com
(5)©Herr Loeffler/Shutterstock.com (6)©Antonio Guillem/Shutterstock.com (7)©cigdem/Shutterstock.com

2 Talk

Pair up with your F/P and take turns asking for help, one by one (problems 1 to 7 above).

5

Group Presentation:
Explore global problems

Can-dos
◎プレゼンテーションソフト（PowerPoint 等）を使って，2分程度のまとまりのある話ができる。
◎自分の発表と前後の発表とを関連づけて，グループとして統一感のある発表ができる。
◎発表後の討論をリードし，問題解決の提示や発展的な議論に導くことができる。

Task 1 — What's going on around the world?

1 Speak up

🔊 24

photo 1   ©Kevin Carter/Sygma Premium/
GettyImages

Your teacher will show the class ⌈photo 1⌉ and ask a few questions.

- What do you see in the photo?
- Do you think the child is alive?
- Where do you think this photo was taken?
- What sort of problems does this photo reflect?
- ...

2 Talk

Pair up with your **S P** and take turns asking each other the questions below.

- Do you think this photograph sends a powerful message?
- What would you do if you walked into this scene?

🔊 25

Task 2 — Describe the picture by filling in the missing words below

In ⌈photo 1⌉ we can see a child (crou   ) down on the ground in a dry, desert-like landscape. The child is extremely (th   ) and appears not to be moving. A vulture stands several meters (be   ) the child, as if waiting. We can guess from this scene that the child is close to death, if not dead already.

Task 3 — What problems are we facing on earth?

1 Talk

1. Match each photo with a global problem from the following list.
2. Discuss the following photos with your **F P**. What problems do you see?

©SpeedKingz/Shutterstock.com ©panitanphoto/Shutterstock.com ©Larina Maria/Shutterstock.com

(   ) (   ) (   )

©nuttawat yotadee/Shutterstock.com ©Keith Tarrier/ Shutterstock.com ©Nicolas Economou/ Shutterstock.com

(   ) (   ) (   )

| pandemic | migrant crisis | poverty |

| nuclear threat | food waste | plastic problem |

Task 4 — Make a list of global problems

1 List

1. Form a team of 4 partners.
2. Sit at your desks in a straight line, front to back, facing the board.
3. If you are sitting at the front of your group, come to the board with a black marker or piece of chalk.
4. Write down a global problem in your group column on the board (Board 1). When you finish, pass the marker or chalk to your group partner sitting behind you.
5. Continue listing global problems on the board, one by one, until your teacher tells you to stop. Try to list problems that are not listed by the other teams.
6. Congratulate the team that lists the largest number of problems.

A	B	C
global warming	pandemic	
migrant crisis	nuclear threat	
poverty	terrorism	
gender equality	endangered animals	
...	...	

Board 1

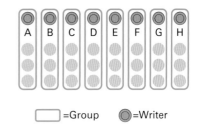

☐=Group   ◎=Writer

Task 5 Prepare a group presentation

1. Choose a global problem to talk about from the lists on the board, and circle the problem (Board 2).

2. Prepare a presentation by filling out the Group Presentation Form (Table 1). Follow the instructions below.
   - Prepare your presentation in the slideshow style (e.g., **PowerPoint**).
   - Each partner talks **for 2 minutes**.
   - Try not to look down at your draft during your presentation.
   - Provide one or two **discussion points** after presenting.

3. (Your teacher might show an example of a presentation.)

4. Give the teacher your Group Presentation Form (Table 1) before the end of class.

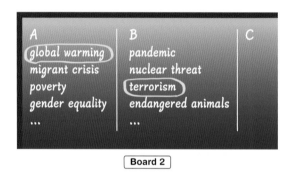

Board 2

Table 1 **Group Presentation Form**
(Turn in a copy of this form to the teacher before the end of class.)

Group:　　Topic　　　　　　　subtitle

Presentation

Presenter	Roles	Contents	Presenter
1	Introduce the presentation and global problem.	• Grab the audience's attention. • Preview the main theme or points. • …	Name _____ Student No. _____
2	Describe and analyze the problem.	• What causes the problem? • What makes it difficult to solve the problem? • Cite statistics or expert opinions. • …	Name _____ Student No. _____
3	Discuss and explore the problem.	• Is there any solution to the problem? • How is the problem relevant to you or the people of Japan? • What can you or the international community do? • …	Name _____ Student No. _____
4	Conclude the presentation.	• Summarize. • Thank the audience. • Make a memorable point at the end. • …	Name _____ Student No. _____

Discussion

Moderator	Lead and develop the discussion.	1. Provide one or two discussion points and ask the audience to think about them for 3 to 5 minutes. 2. Ask a few groups to report their views. Lead a discussion between the groups. 3. Wrap up the discussion.	Name _____ Student No. _____

Important:

✓ Each presenter chooses a role and talks for at least 2 minutes.

✓ Each group provides one or two discussion points after the presentation and leads the discussion.

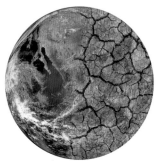

©BeautifulPicture/Shutterstock.com

Your part of the presentation:

Topic   subtitle

Language 1 **Useful expressions for presentations**

❖ For all presenters

🔊
27

Emphasize your points

❏ I would like to draw your attention to ...

❏ As you can see here, ...

❏ Note that ...

❏ Now let's look at ...

❏ Let's consider ...

❏ Let me move on to my next point, ...

❏ Before we move on, does anyone have any questions?

❏ If you have any questions, I'll be happy to answer them now.

❏ I will come back to that point at the end.

❏ We will come back to this point later.

Explain the slides

❏ Here you see ... / Here we have ...

❏ If you look at ..., you will see that ...

❖ For presenter 1 ([Table 1])

Start your presentation

❑ Hello everyone, my name is …

❑ Good morning/afternoon/evening, my name is … I am …

❑ Today we are going to talk about …

Outline your presentation

❑ Here is an outline of our presentation.

❑ First, we will briefly introduce …

❑ Second, we will describe …

❑ Third, we will explain …

❑ Then we will finish with a brief conclusion.

❑ Let me start with the introduction.

❑ Our talk is divided into four (five) parts.

❑ We would like to begin by … Then … Finally, …

❑ First, … Next, … Finally, …

❖ For presenter 4 ([Table 1])

Conclude your presentation

❑ Let me conclude our presentation.

❑ To sum up, …

❑ In conclusion, …

❑ We would like to conclude by saying …

❑ That concludes our presentation. Thank you for listening.

❑ That's all we have to say. Thank you for your attention.

Presentation day

❑ Materials to prepare

〈Students〉

- a USB flash memory or laptop computer for each group, and a draft of the presentation, if necessary

〈Teacher〉

- A PC and projector screen (usually equipped in the classroom)
- Feedback Forms (p. 35)
- A remote controller, if available
- Feedback Envelopes (one for each presenter) (photo 2)

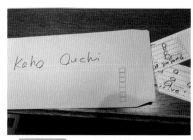
photo 2 Feedback Envelope

❑ Be seated in groups (Board 3).

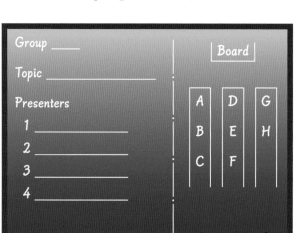

Board 3

Asking questions

🔊
28

❏ If I could make one comment on …

❏ Could you go back to the slide showing …?

❏ I have a question about the slide on …

❏ Am I correct in assuming that …?

❏ If I understood you correctly, you said that …

❏ I have a question about …

Clarifying

❏ Does that answer your question?

❏ I hope that answers your question.

❏ Am I making sense here?

❏ Am I making myself clear?

❏ Let me know if I'm being unclear.

❏ Sorry. I meant to say …

❏ Let me correct myself. I meant to say …

Feedback Form				
Presenter　　　　　　　　　Evaluator (your name)				
The speech was interesting.	1	2	3	4
The speaker delivered the speech in a firm, confident voice.	1	2	3	4
The speaker kept eye contact with the audience.	1	2	3	4
Overall impression	Poor	Fair	Good	Excellent
Free comments (Required)				

1 Strongly disagree　　2 Somewhat disagree　　3 Somewhat agree　　4 Strongly agree

Chapter 6

Human migration

Can-dos
◉日本の難民・移民政策を欧米のそれと比較検討し，今後の方向性を考えられる。
◉内容を要約したメモを見ながら，事実を伝えることができる。

Task 1　Define the terms

Match the four terms below with definitions a) to d).　🔊 29

| foreign workers | immigrants | refugees | asylum seekers |

a) people who have been forced to leave their countries, often because of war or for political or religious reasons.　(　　　)

b) people who have sought international protection but have yet to be granted official refugee status.　(　　　)

c) people who leave one country to permanently settle in another.　(　　　)

d) people who work in a country without being citizens of that country.　(　　　)

Task 2　What's happening in Germany?

1 **Read aloud**　Pair up with your SP and read the text aloud sentence by sentence.

🔊 30

[1] We sailed to Greece in a small fishing boat, passed through Serbia into Hungary in the back of a truck, crossed the border into Austria on foot at midnight, and reached Germany by train. We were just three — a father, son, and daughter — among the almost 300 Syrians who arrived in Munich rail station that day. Our welcome was warm. A group of volunteers at the station handed us sandwiches, bottled water, and pamphlets about life in Germany. An elderly woman led us to a counter and helped us fill out paperwork for our first home in the country, a reception center for asylum seekers on the outskirts of town.

[2] Our room in the reception center was furnished with bunk beds and a kitchenette. The German government provided everyone in the center with food, spending money, and language lessons. We also received donations — second-hand clothes, an old tablet, toys for the children — from kindly Germans in the neighbourhood.

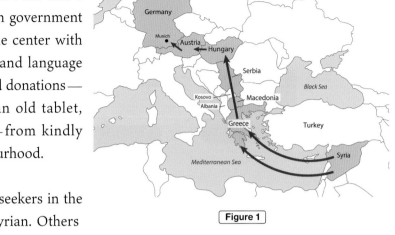

Figure 1

[3] Most of the asylum seekers in the reception center were Syrian. Others came from Albania and Kosovo. Our family, like many others from Syria, had been devastated by the violence at home. Parents were widowed; children were orphaned.

[4] We stayed at the center for 13 months, waiting for the German government to process our asylum request. I wept when our acceptance came through. We were assigned to live in North Rhine-Westphalia, one of Germany's most affluent states. Our residence permit was valid for three years. For the first three months I was forbidden to work, but our family continued to receive food, housing, and spending money. As residents we were qualified to receive the same social benefits as Germans.

[5] The Albanian and Kosovan asylum seekers we had known at the reception center were not so lucky. Germany rejected their applications for asylum because they had come from 'safe countries of origin' — countries to which they could safely return. They were asked to leave Germany within 30 days. In Germany they hoped to escape joblessness and poverty. The violence we left behind in Syria was far worse.

2 🎧 **Listen and repeat**

3 **Check your understanding** Ask each other the questions below.

31

- What did the asylum seeker and his family receive from kindly neighbors living near the reception center?
- What did the German government provide for them for the first three months after their asylum request was approved?
- What were the failed applicants from Albania and Kosovo asked to do?

4 Fill in the blanks in Figure 2

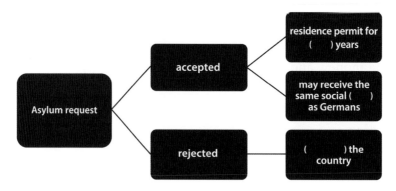

Figure 2 The asylum request process in Germany

5 Explain

Pair up with your F/P and take turns explaining the procedure for processing an asylum request shown in Figure 2 . Use your own words.

6 Discuss Ask each other the questions below.

- Why do you think Germany accepts refugees?
- What sort of problems might arise between Germans and asylum seekers?
- Would you agree to accept asylum seekers if you were German?

Task 3 What countries accommodate refugees?

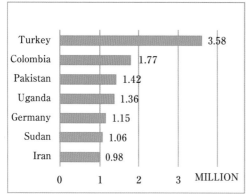

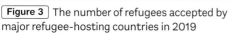

Figure 3 The number of refugees accepted by major refugee-hosting countries in 2019
(Global Trends: Forced Displacement in 2019, UNHCR)

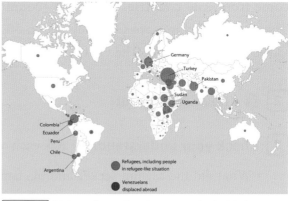

Figure 4 Major refugee-hosting countries in 2019
(Global Trends: Forced Displacement in 2019, UNHCR)

1 Check your understanding

Look at [Figure 3] and [Figure 4]. Pair up with your D̲P̲ and ask each other the questions below.

- What country receives the most refugees?
- How many refugees does that country receive?
- Which country on the list do you think is most developed?

2 Talk Pair up with your S̲P̲ and ask each other the questions below.

- What else can you notice from looking at [Figure 3] and [Figure 4] ?
- Why do you think Turkey receives so many refugees?
- Why do you think Colombia comes second in [Figure 3] ?

34

3 Fill in the blanks (a) to (d) in the passage below.

[Figure 3] shows the seven countries hosting the largest numbers of refugees in 2019. The developing regions shoulder a disproportionately large responsibility for hosting displaced populations. (a) hosted the greatest number of refugees, 3.6 million. Ninety-eight percent of the refugees living in (a) were from Syria, a war-torn country that ranked last on the Global Peace Index from 2016 to 2018. (b) hosted the second-largest refugee population, with 1.77 million refugees from Venezuela, a failed state whose citizens live under the constant threat of violence, often without food, medicine, or other essential services. (c) hosted the third-largest refugee population, most of whom originated in Afghanistan. Uganda and Sudan rank fourth and sixth, respectively, accepting refugees mostly from South Sudan, a country torn by civil war.

Almost all of the nearly 1 million refugees living in (d), the seventh-ranking country, originated from neighboring Afghanistan, and the remainder came from Iraq. When people flee a country to escape conflict and persecution, they often go to places close to their home countries.

Germany is unique as the only developed country among the seven listed. Other developed countries accept refugees, but not nearly on the same scale. The United States of America received 30,000 refugees in 2019, a rather small number for an economic superpower. Japan, a country known for its tight immigration policy, received only 44 refugees in 2019, a tiny fraction of the 10,375 people who applied.

4 **Check your understanding** Pair up with your $\boxed{\substack{\text{F}\\\text{P}}}$ and ask each other the questions below.

- How many people who applied for refugee status in Japan were accepted in 2019?
- How many refugees were accepted by the US in 2019?

5 **Build your vocabulary**

🔊 35

Table 1

✓	English	Japanese
☐	food, medicine, or other essential services	
☐	rank fourth	
☐	flee a country	
☐	escape conflict and persecution	
☐	economic superpower	
☐	tight immigration policy	
☐	accept refugees	

1) Translate the terms above from English to Japanese.

2) Memorize

① 🔤 with your $\boxed{\text{S}\,\text{P}}$.

Winner: Translate the first phrase above into Japanese and say it out loud.

Loser: 📖 and translate the phrase back into English.

② Do the same for the other phrases, checking the boxes ☑ as you go.

③ 🔄

3) Respond

① 📖

② Your teacher will read out the words and phrases in Japanese, one by one. Work with the rest of the class to translate the Japanese phrases back into English.

6 **Discuss** Pair up with your $\boxed{\substack{\text{D}\\\text{P}}}$ and ask each other the questions below.

- Why do you think the US accepts such a small number of refugees?
- Do you think Japan should accept more refugees in the future?

- 980,000   (   )
- 3,600,000 (   )
- 341,711   (   )

Optional task

1 Research and present

1) Find out about Ms. Sadako Ogata.
2) Form a group of four (two pairs) and present your reports.

2 Talk

Pair up with your S P and take turns asking the question, "What was her message for the world and Japan?"

©UNHCR

Task 4   What's happening in the US?

1 🎧 Listen and repeat

🔊 36

[1] US immigration policy is based on three principles. First, the policy gives priority to close relatives of US citizens and the relatives of immigrants already in the country. Second, the policy gives priority to persons with occupations, skills, and capital that will benefit the US economy. This latter policy may contribute to a loss of highly skilled and professionally trained persons in developing countries, a phenomenon called the "brain drain." The brain drain may not be entirely negative, as some people who are "drained" from their countries return home with newly gained education, skills, and experience from abroad. Third, the US immigration policy requires eligible immigrants to meet a long list of personal qualifications, such as good health, a lack of a criminal background, and sufficient economic resources. The US also issues "non-immigrant" visas to persons visiting the country for specific purposes such as tourism or business, university study, consulting, and temporary employment. A range of people from around the world are thus welcomed into the US through two different channels.

[2] The US government imposed greater control of refugee and visa applications after thousands of people were murdered in the September 11 terrorist attacks in New York City in 2001. Refugee admissions to the US dropped sharply just after the attacks, from nearly 80,000 in 2001 to roughly 27,000 in 2002. The number of incoming refugees steadily rose for the next 14 years, reaching a peak of about 85,000 in 2016.

[3] Donald J Trump, the former US president, sought political gain by fueling anti-immigrant sentiment in the American public. In his campaign for office in 2016, Trump promised to build a wall across the southern border to protect America from what he called an "invasion" of migrants flooding in from Mexico and Central America. Critics charged that Trump's policy responded to "imaginary facts" at the border.

[4] The United States is a young country built by immigrants. Over many periods of their history, the American public have valued immigrants for the diversity, culture, expertise, and sense of hope they bring. In 2021, the world is watching to see if Donald Trump's successor, President Joseph Biden, will be able to restore a more balanced stance toward immigration and a recognition of the benefits that immigrants bring to a national culture and economy.

2 **Read aloud** Pair up with your F/P and take turns reading the text aloud, sentence by sentence.

3 **Check your understanding** Ask each other the following questions.
- What type of immigrants are more likely to be admitted into the US (paragraph [1])?
- What is the "brain drain" problem? (paragraph [1]).
- Why did the US government tighten its control of refugee and visa applications in the early 2000s (paragraph [2])?

4 **Fill in the blanks**

Read paragraph [1] to fill in the blanks in Figure 5 below.

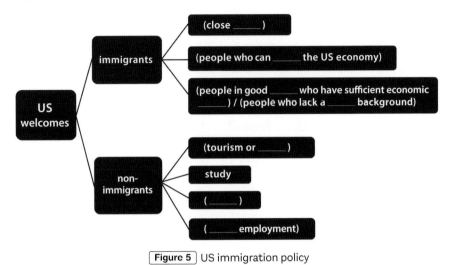

Figure 5 US immigration policy

Optional task
Explain

Talk about the US immigration policy according to the information given in Figure 5 .

① 🙋 with your D P .

Winner : Begin your talk by stating, "The US welcomes people into the country as immigrants or as non-immigrants." Do not look at the passage.

Loser : Listen.

② ●⇄●

5 **Talk** Pair up with your S P and ask each other the questions below.

- Do you think you have skills that could benefit the US economy?
- Would someone miss your skills and expertise if you emigrated to another country?
- Have you ever conducted a crime that would prevent you from immigrating to the US? Please be honest!
- Would you like to be a US citizen? Why or why not?
- What positive things have immigrants brought with them into the US?

Choose or be chosen?

 Can-dos ◉移民や難民の受け入れを通じて，他者との共生と日本の持続可能性を志向できる。
◉論点を記したメモを見ながら，意見や主張を伝え合うことができる。

Task 1 **Where are they from?**

1 **Speak up** Your teacher will ask the class the questions below.
39

- When you see a foreign worker in a convenience store, construction site, or somewhere else in Japan, do you start up a chat?
- Where do you think foreign workers are from?

2 **Talk**

Pair up with your **S P** and ask each other the questions above.

Task 2 **Should Japan accept more immigrants and refugees?**

1 **Speak up and share**

① Your teacher will ask, *"Should Japan accept more immigrants and refugees?"* Answer the question and give your reasons.

② Your teacher will pick a few students and ask them to share their views with the rest of the class. As they do, the teacher will jot down their ideas.

③ Have a debate with your **S P** on the benefits and disadvantages of accepting immigrants and refugees.

④ Repeat step ③ with your **D P** .

Reject	Accept
Nanami: 　crimes will increase	Taiga: 　want to help them
Shohei: 　language barrier	Natsuki: 　boost Japan's economy
………	………
…………………	…………………

Board 1

Task 3　How many refugees does Japan accept?

Refugee applications and acceptances in Japan

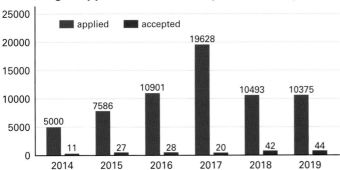

Figure 1 The number of the people who applied to enter Japan as refugees, and the number of people accepted

(Source; Ministry of Justice, 2020)

1 Choose

Which of the following statements is true according to Figure 1.

a) There has never been a decrease in the number of asylum seekers applying to enter Japan.

b) Hundreds of thousands of people applied to enter Japan between 2014 and 2016.

c) More people applied to enter Japan as refugees in 2017 compared to the year before.

d) In every year shown, more than 1 percent of the people who applied to enter Japan were accepted.

2 Describe Look at Figure 2 and fill in the blanks.

(M　　　) than half of the German, Japanese, and American respondents believe that immigrants fill useful jobs in their countries. Compared to the German respondents, (fe　　　) of the Japanese and Americans answered "no" to the survey question. The results suggest that Germans tend to be less

Do immigrants fill useful jobs in your country?

Figure 2　(Source; World Values Survey Wave 7)

positive about immigrants than the Japanese and Americans. Nearly (ha　　　) of the Turks polled believe that immigrants do not fill useful jobs, while only a quarter of the Turks say that they do. Turks seem to be the (lea　　　) positive about the economic contributions of immigrants in their country.

45

Chapter 7

3 **Analyze and talk**

Pair up with your FP and take turns asking each other the questions below.

- The findings in Turkey are quite different from those in Japan and the US. What do you think could explain the difference?
- More than half of the Japanese polled agree that immigrants fill useful jobs. Does this result seem consistent with the data on Japan shown in Figure 1 (p.45)?
- Do you think that immigrants fill useful jobs in Japan's workforce? Explain.

Task 4   **What are the pros and cons?**

1 **Read aloud**

⟳ with your SP.

Winner : Play the part of Ryo.

Loser : Play the part of Sakura.

1 Sakura: Hi, Ryo. Have you finished your essay on immigration yet?

2 Ryo: Uhm... no, but I know what I want to write. I'm against accepting more immigrants. More foreigners coming into Japan would impose a further burden on the economy, which is already doing badly. Many immigrants would lack the money to pay their taxes, which would shift a financial burden to the Japanese people. That would be unfair. I also fear that public safety, a point of pride in Japan, would be at risk. The immigrants or refugees might commit crimes to get money. They would also be frustrated by their wages, which would be lower than what the average Japanese person receives. Look at the many conflicts and disputes between immigrants and locals in Germany and France. The threat of terrorist attacks would rise, too. And the immigrants would have a tough time getting used to the Japanese way of life, customs, and unwritten rules.

3 Sakura: I disagree! You seem to have many biases against immigrants. My friends from Vietnam and Brazil study hard, behave decently, and are better disciplined than typical Japanese students. Japan is an aging society facing a shortage of workers. We Japanese will be unable to maintain our current prosperity and economic growth unless we do something about our shrinking population. Immigrants can compensate for the shortage of workers, especially in fields such as construction, caregiving, and food service. And immigrants with advanced degrees in science and engineering bring with them expertise to strengthen Japan's industries and economy.

4 Ryo: I agree that people with high-level expertise have something to offer. But who knows how long we will need construction workers, convenience store clerks, or caregiving workers? Sooner or later, AI and robots will take over those jobs. In ten years or so, I predict that workers will no longer be needed in those industries. We are already paying for our groceries using automatic cashiers in supermarkets.

5 Sakura: But not all jobs can be replaced with AI or robots, especially in fields that require human-to-human communication and experience. Nursing and caregiving are good examples. People in those professions will be in higher demand as our society ages. Apart from that, Japan should set an example as a leading developed country in the global community by helping people in need. After all, the prosperity and peace we enjoy at home in Japan strongly depends on stable and peaceful conditions abroad. We live in an interdependent world. Japan will hurt itself if it becomes too self-serving.

6 Ryo: What you are saying is true in principle but doesn't work in practice. Accepting immigrants or refugees would cause serious problems that we could never hope to solve. Even now our unemployment rate is increasing. A sense of uncertainty and unrest is spreading, and our security is about to decline. Japan has already contributed to world peace and the well-being of people in other countries by providing humanitarian support and huge amounts of money through ODA and international organizations such as the United Nations.

7 Sakura: Ryo, you seem to forget that Japan itself will be unable to manage unless it takes immediate and concrete actions to keep its own society from shrinking. I admit that some of the problems you point out are real. We need to shift our focus from whether Japan should accept immigrants to how Japan can welcome them, help them adjust to life here, and encourage them to contribute to a better future for our society. Many Japanese, even the government, seem to believe they can choose who to accept from overseas. The reality is the reverse. It is the immigrants from overseas who do the choosing. Japan, to them, is just one of several options.

2 🎧 **Listen and repeat**

42

Answer questions 1) to 8) below.

Questions

1) Which of the following statements does Ryo *not* make in remark **2** ?

   a) Immigrants are likely to threaten Japan's safety.

   b) Accepting immigrants is likely to burden the Japanese economy.

   c) Immigrants find life in Japan difficult to manage.

   d) Accepting immigrants is likely to promote the aging of Japanese society.

2) What benefit will accepting more immigrants bring according to Sakura's remark **3** ?

   a) Immigrant students are likely to improve the study habits of Japanese youth.

   b) Immigrants can help solve the workforce shortage.

   c) Immigrants in Japan will promote friendships with Vietnam and Brazil.

   d) Immigrants will make Japanese society more diverse.

3) Why does Sakura mention Vietnam and Brazil in remark **3** ?

   a) To counter Ryo's arguments.

   b) To suggest that those countries have problems similar to Japan's.

   c) To show how wonderful Japan is by comparison.

   d) To argue that Vietnam and Brazil will one day be richer than Japan.

4) Why does Ryo mention automatic cashiers in remark **4** ?

   a) To argue that robots will never be smart enough to replace cashiers.

   b) To illustrate why he thinks fewer workers will be needed in the future.

   c) To emphasize how advanced AI is.

   d) To imply that convenient stores will soon disappear.

5) What debate strategy is Sakura using in remark **5** ?

   a) She is claiming that Ryo's argument is irrelevant.

   b) She is providing more reliable data.

   c) She is introducing testimony.

   d) She is pointing out an exception.

6) What does Sakura say about Japan's responsibilities in remark **5** ?

   a) Japan has fulfilled its responsibilities overall.

   b) Japan should let other countries take care of their own responsibilities.

   c) Japan should set an example as a leading country by helping people overseas.

   d) Japan is unable to sufficiently fulfil its responsibilities.

7) Why does Ryo mention ODA and the UN in remark **6** ?

    a) To suggest that Japan has already made adequate contributions to the world.

    b) To demonstrate that cooperation is the key to helping developing countries.

    c) To suggest how important humanitarian aid is.

    d) To indicate how many people in the world need help.

8) What is the main point Sakura makes in remark **7** ?

    a) Immigrants enrich Japan by bringing their diverse cultures.

    b) Accepting immigrants is very risky.

    c) Individual decisions are more important than national decisions.

    d) The Japanese need to think about immigrants in a new way.

4 Build your vocabulary

Table 1

	✓	English	Japanese
2	☐	impose a burden on	
	☐	pay one's taxes	
	☐	be at risk	
	☐	commit crimes	
	☐	conflicts and disputes	
3	☐	behave decently	
	☐	be well disciplined	
	☐	the aging of society	
	☐	shortage of workers	
	☐	prosperity and economic growth	
	☐	compensate for	
	☐	construction, caregiving, and food service	
4	☐	sooner or later	
	☐	take over	
5	☐	higher-level skills	
	☐	be in higher demand	
	☐	depend on	
6	☐	humanitarian support	
7	☐	take immediate and concrete actions	

1) Translate the terms above from English to Japanese.

2) Memorize

① 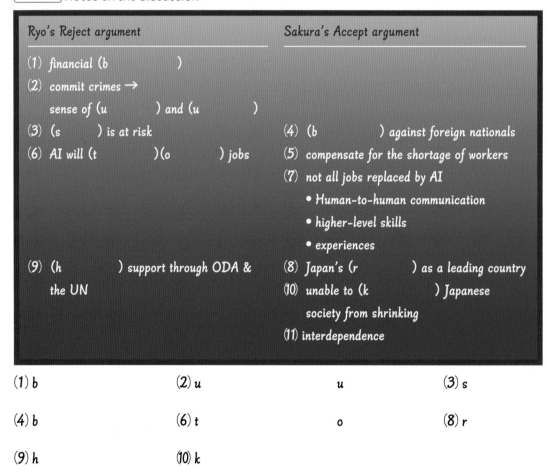 S P

    Winner: Translate the first phrase above into Japanese and say it out loud.

    Loser : and translate the phrase back into English.

② Do the same for the other phrases, checking the boxes ☑ as you go.

③

3) Respond

①

② Your teacher will read out the words and phrases in Japanese, one by one. Work with the rest of the class to translate the Japanese phrases back into English.

5 **Summarize** the discussion between Ryo and Sakura in ⌈ Board 2 ⌉.

① Your teacher will copy ⌈ Board 2 ⌉.

② Volunteer to come to the board and fill in the blanks.

⌈ Board 2 ⌉ Notes on the discussion

Ryo's Reject argument	Sakura's Accept argument
(1) financial (b)	
(2) commit crimes →	
sense of (u) and (u)	
(3) (s) is at risk	(4) (b) against foreign nationals
(6) AI will (t)(o) jobs	(5) compensate for the shortage of workers
	(7) not all jobs replaced by AI
	• Human-to-human communication
	• higher-level skills
	• experiences
(9) (h) support through ODA &	(8) Japan's (r) as a leading country
the UN	(10) unable to (k) Japanese
	society from shrinking
	(11) interdependence

(1) b   (2) u   u   (3) s

(4) b   (6) t   o   (8) r

(9) h   (10) k

6 Role play

① 🖼 and 🎭 with your D̲P̲ .

Winner: Play the part of Ryo.

Loser : Play the part of Sakura.

② Have a debate with your partner. If you are Ryo, argue points (1), (2), (3), (6), and (9) in ⌞Board 2⌟. If you are Sakura, argue points (4), (5), (7), (8), (10), and (11).

7 Discuss

① Freely discuss the following question with your S̲P̲: "Should Japan accept more refugees?"

② 🔁 and continue the discussion.

Wrap-up

How can Japan welcome immigrants to help them live comfortably and contribute to Japanese society?

① Share your opinions about the question above with your F̲P̲.

② Share your opinions with the class.

③ Write out your opinion.

Chapter 8

Who are the *Barumbans*?

Can-dos
◉異なるコミュニティに対する自分自身の無理解や，無意識に気づくことができる。
◉話し合った内容を要約し，報告できる。

1 Procedure

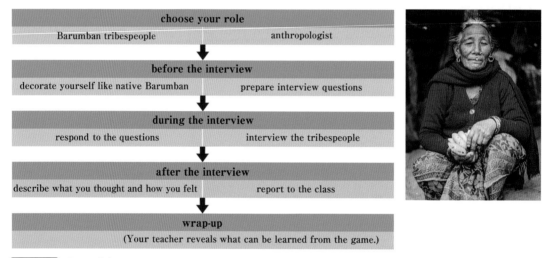

choose your role	
Barumban tribespeople	anthropologist

↓

before the interview	
decorate yourself like native Barumban	prepare interview questions

↓

during the interview	
respond to the questions	interview the tribespeople

↓

after the interview	
describe what you thought and how you felt	report to the class

↓

wrap-up
(Your teacher reveals what can be learned from the game.)

Table 1 Flow of the game

2 Choose your role and prepare

Volunteer to be a member of the Barumban tribe. About one in five students in the class should volunteer. The other students will be anthropologists.

☐ Barumban tribespeople
　① Move to a different room with your teacher (or get together in the hallway just outside the classroom if no other rooms are available).
　② See the "**For the Barumbans**" worksheet.

☐ Anthropologists
　① Stay in the classroom and form a group of 4 students. Choose a group leader.
　② See the "**For the Anthropologists**" worksheet (p.53).
　③ Prepare your interview questions for the Barumbans.

For the Anthropologists (the Barumban tribes people must not see this page)

Mission

Find out what Barumbans are like.

©ProStockStudio/Shutterstock.com

1 | Before the Interviews

① Form a group with four of your neighbors and choose a leader.

Group Members

- _____ (team leader)

- _____

- _____

- _____

- (_____)

② Move the tables and chairs into the arrangement shown in [Figure 1] (p. 54) and take a seat in your group.

③ Prepare questions to ask the Barumban tribespeople. Your goal is to learn about the Barumbans and their culture. Remember that the Barumbans only understand Yes/No questions in English. You might ask, for example:

- Do you eat rice?
- Do you hold general elections?
- ...

2 Begin the interview

① Meet with one of the Barumban tribespeople for a 3-minute interview (Photo 2).
② Do the same two more times with the other Barumbans (Figure 1).
③ Take notes during the interviews to prepare for your class report afterwards.

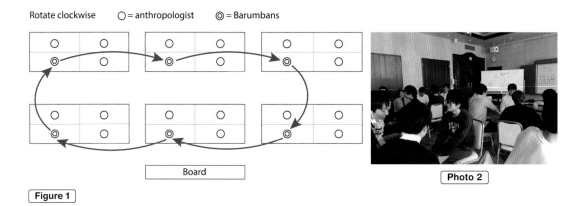

Photo 2

Figure 1

3 After the Interview

① Based on their interview responses, discuss the Barumbans' personalities, culture, everyday customs, religious beliefs, and economic and political systems.
② Choose a reporter to share the insights of your team with the rest of the class.

Reporter's notes: Reporter's name [   ]

The Barumbans are

③ Welcome the Barumban tribespeople back into the classroom.
④ Take turns reporting your findings to the class.
⑤ Listen to the Barumban tribespeople express their thoughts and feelings in English. (They now have the ability to speak it.)

4 Ending

① Listen to your teacher reveal the purpose of this game.

② Reset the tables and chairs.

Chapter 9

Presumptions: Pink or blue

Can-dos ◉他者の思い込みや先入観によって，違和感や差別を感じた経験を共有し，伝えることができる。

Task 1　**Have you ever been treated unfairly or unequally?**

1　**Read in silence**

① Pair up with your S P .

② 🪨 .

　　Winner : Read the passage *Pink or Blue?* to yourself.

　　Loser :　Read *Swimming School*.

Pink or Blue? (passage for 🪨 winners)

　　When I was 12 years old, our teacher gave us T-shirts. The shirts came in two colors, pink and blue.

　　"Blue for boys, pink for girls," the teacher said.

　　My classmates and teacher thought that boys looked good in blue and girls looked good in pink. I loved the blue ones. This was the first time I thought about gender discrimination.

Akane

Swimming School (passage for 🪨 losers)

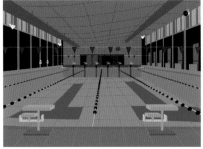

©magnusz28/Shutterstock.com

　　Back in elementary school, I went to a swimming school once a week. One day the school held a competition. The instructor told us that we would be separated into two groups: one for the faster kids, the other for the slower kids. The instructor assigned me to the slower group. I've hated swimming ever since. I still wonder why we all couldn't have competed together.

Kei

2 Retell

①

② 🎲 to decide who goes first.

③ Tell each other the stories you have just read. Exchange comments and suggestions after each story.

④ 📖 and confirm the stories.

3 Share Ask each other the questions below.

🔊 45

- What issue does Akane describe in *Pink or Blue*?
- Do you think Akane's teacher was wrong in assuming that girls like pink and boys like blue?
- Do you think Kei's swimming instructor was being unfair?

Task 2

1 Read in silence

① Pair up with your [F/P].

② 🎲

Winner : Read the passage *Father* to yourself.

Loser :　Read *Locker Room* to yourself.

Father (passage for 🎲 winners)

🔊 46

　I grew up in a family without a father. Some of my classmates and teachers in high school pitied me. They thought I was lacking something as a person and needed special help. A father, they assumed, was essential for a person's development as a human being. While my mother and grandparents don't have much money, they are loving and supportive. They have always provided everything I need. Being fatherless has never been a problem for me. I think people from single-parent households are judged unfairly.

Natsuki

Locker Room (passage for 🎲 losers)

　In junior high school I joined the basketball club. The school had only one locker room, for girls. So after school, I had to change clothes in the gym in front of the girls. That was embarrassing. I wanted to change in a locker room for boys only.

Hayato

©shutter_tonko/Shutterstock.com

2 Retell

①

② 🔲 to decide who goes first.

③ Tell each other the stories you have just read. Exchange comments and suggestions after each story.

④ 📖 and confirm the stories.

3 Share Ask each other the question below.

- Have you ever had an experience similar to Natsuki's or Hayato's?

Task 3

1 Read in silence

① Pair up with your D P .

② 🔲

Winner: Read the passage *Dyed Hair* to yourself.

Loser :　Read *A Waiter* to yourself.

Dyed Hair (passage for 🔲 winners)

🔊 47

One day, back in high school, my homeroom teacher examined my hair.

"Your hair looks dyed," she said. "Dyeing your hair is against the school rules."

Most Japanese people have black hair. My hair has always been a natural brown. Never in my life have I dyed it. My homeroom teacher demanded that I bring my mother to school to assure her that my hair was naturally brown.

©tibori / Shutterstock.com

"Do I have to?" I asked.

"Yes, you have to."

So along came my mother to speak to the teacher. "My son was born with beautiful brown hair," she said. "He would never dye it."

Kozo

A Waiter (passage for losers)

I studied abroad in London for two weeks over the summer break in my second year of high school. One morning my classmates and I walked around the city to see the sights, stopping by places like the Tower of London and Big Ben. At lunchtime we went into a restaurant. The waiter showed us to our table, making no effort to appear welcoming or polite.

©Pretty Vectors/Shutterstock.com

Over lunch we noticed that the waiter was unfriendly only to us. He smiled warmly to all of the other customers. We suspected that he was biased against us because we were young and Asian.

As we rose from our seats to leave, the waiter rushed to our table to thank us with a warm smile. He probably hoped we would leave a good tip.

Shutaro

2 Retell

①
② to decide who goes first.
③ Tell each other the stories you have just read. Exchange comments and suggestions after each story.
④ and confirm the stories.

3 Share Ask each other the questions below.

🔊
48

- Shouldn't high school students be allowed to dye their hair?
- Have you ever had an experience similar to Shutaro's?

Task 4   What about you?

1 Share

① Recall a time when you felt discriminated against or treated unfairly.

② Take 3 minutes to prepare a story about that experience.

③ Pair up with your S P and 🙋 to decide who goes first.

④ Tell your stories.

2 Write and speak

① Take 10 minutes to write out the story you told in ①.

② 🙋 to decide who goes first.

③ Tell the story. Maintain eye contact with your S P .

Discuss your opinions

① Check the boxes ☑ in [Table 1] that best describe your opinions.

② Discuss your opinions with your **F** **P** .

③ [icon] and discuss your opinions.

[Table 1] Opinions

🔊 49

Statement	Strongly agree	Agree	Somewhat agree	Somewhat disagree	Disagree	Strongly disagree
Boys look good in blue and girls look good in pink.	❑	❑	❑	❑	❑	❑
High school students should be allowed to dye their hair.	❑	❑	❑	❑	❑	❑
People with university degrees are smarter than people without them.	❑	❑	❑	❑	❑	❑
*Only children are selfish.	❑	❑	❑	❑	❑	❑
People with disabilities contribute less to society than people without disabilities.	❑	❑	❑	❑	❑	❑
People who often change jobs lack perseverance and grit.	❑	❑	❑	❑	❑	❑
People who divorce lack perseverance and grit.	❑	❑	❑	❑	❑	❑
Single people value freedom more than married people.	❑	❑	❑	❑	❑	❑
Couples with children are happier than couples without them.	❑	❑	❑	❑	❑	❑

*An only child is a person with no siblings.

Chapter 10 Gender equality and roles

Can-dos

◉文化や宗教固有の価値観を相対化し，新しい時代のジェンダーのあり方を志向できる。

◉グラフから読み取れる情報を，比較表現を用いて伝えることができる。

Task 1 — What would you do?

1 Talk

Imagine you are a 32-year old woman working full time at a company. You and your partner are expecting a baby.

① Pair up with your ⓢⓟ and take turns asking the question, "Would you take childcare leave if you had the opportunity?"

② 🔁 and discuss the above question.

2 Share your preferences with the class

Task 2 — How evenly do Japanese couples share housework?

1 Guess

Figure 1 below charts the additional hours wives spend on house chores, compared to their husbands, in four countries (Japan, France, Finland, and Taiwan). Work with your ⓢⓟ to guess the country represented by each bar.

A (   )   B (   )   C (   )   D (   )

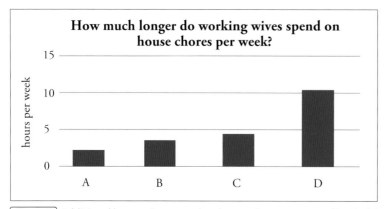

Figure 1 Additional hours wives spend on house chores compared to their husbands

2 Talk

Share what you find surprising or new about Figure 1 .

Task 3   Do Japanese women make better professionals than men?

1 Talk

① Pair up with your F/P and share what you find surprising or new about Figure 2 .

② Ask each other the question, "Why do you think Japanese women are falling behind in the attainment of professional qualifications?"

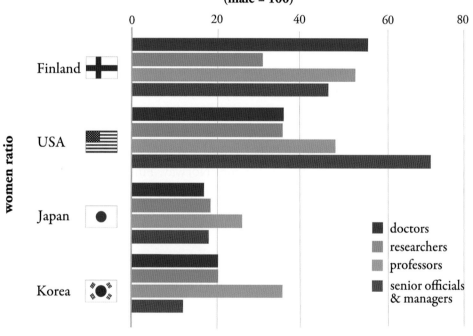

Ratio of women in four professions across four countries (male = 100)

doctors
researchers
professors
senior officials & managers

Figure 2 (source: Global Gender Gap Report (2020), World Economic Forum)

2 Speak up and share

① Your teacher will ask, "Is gender equality advancing in Japan?" Volunteer to answer.

② Pair up with your D/P and share your opinions.

Task 4 — Is gender equality advancing?

1 Listen and read

① 🎧 Listen and repeat

② Read aloud Pair up with your ⓢⓟ and take turns reading the text aloud, sentence by sentence.

🔊
50

[1] The United Nations General Assembly adopted the eight Millennium Development Goals (MDGs) back in 2000. All 191 UN member states and all of the world's leading development organizations declared their commitment to work toward the achievement of the eight MDGs by the target year of 2015. The third goal, MDG 3, called for the promotion of gender equality and the empowerment of women. Unlike conventional goals, the MDGs were to be achieved in quantitatively defined steps, year by year. Under the agreed process for MDG 3, every country was to be held accountable for achieving its commitments to gender equality. When the target year of 2015 was reached, the UN General Assembly set the seventeen Sustainable Development Goals (SDGs), a new set of goals to be completed by the year 2030. SDG 5 replaced MDG 3 as the gender-focused development goal.

[2] According to WEF (World Economic Forum) statistics as of 2020, gender equality efforts have made the most progress in Iceland, Norway, Finland, and Sweden, in that order. Progress has been the weakest in Yemen, followed by Iraq, Pakistan, and Syria. ⸢Figure 3⸥ illustrates the relative difference in the five criteria between men and women in Finland, the US, Japan, and Pakistan. The key indicators for the five criteria are wage equality for similar work (economic participation), professional and technical workers (economic opportunity), women in parliament (political empowerment), enrollment in tertiary education (educational attainment), and healthy life expectancy (health and well-being). Finland, the US, Japan, and Pakistan rank 3rd, 53rd, 121st, and 151st, respectively out of the 153 countries rated for gender equality achievements.

③ Check your understanding: Ask each other the following questions.

Paragraph [1]

- What made the MDGs unique?
- What replaced the MDGs after 2015?
- What are the SDGs?
- What is the aim of SDG 5?

Paragraph [2]

- What country has made the most progress in achieving gender equality?
- What country has been the least successful?

2 **Analyze and talk** Look at Figure 3, and answer the following questions.

- Point out three criteria where Japan has fallen far behind Finland and the US.
- In what criterion has Japan been the least successful in gender equality?
  Name a few Japanese female politicians.
- In what criterion do the four countries rank almost the same in gender equality?

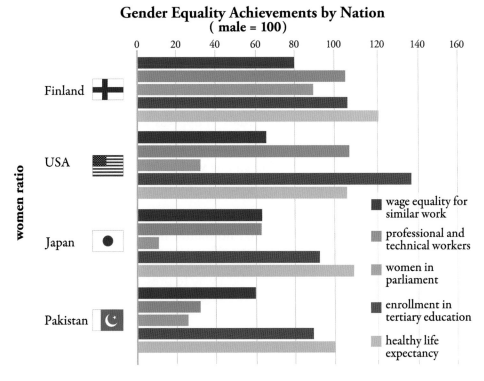

Figure 3 Gender equality achievements by nation
(Global Gender Gap Report (2020), World Economic Forum)

3 Discuss

Do you think gender equality is advancing around the world? Discuss with your D P .

Task 5 — Cultural justification?

1 Read aloud

① Pair up with your and take turns reading the sentences below.

② 🎧 Listen and repeat.

③ Take turns reading the sentences again.

🔊
53

[1] Women and girls in some parts of the world are denied their basic human needs. Born into cultures or religions where women are valued less than men, they may be forced into labor or early marriages. Many are deprived of education, which limits their opportunities to earn money outside of their homes. The denial of a person's basic human needs is sometimes considered a cultural or religious practice that outsiders from other cultures have no right to judge. Is there ever a cultural or religious justification for violating a person's fundamental human rights?

[2] In some cases, religious customs and rituals to oppress women have emerged long after the religions themselves were founded. Opposition to strong women has been a common stance in Christianity and Buddhism, as well as in Islam. Some conservative Christians believe that women should be denied institutional strength or authority in church. Buddhists, who many believe to be more egalitarian in their faith, insist that a nun* must always respect and obey a monk, no matter how inexperienced the monk may be. Women receive unequal treatment in many different cultures and religions of the world. Denying the rights of women may be a way to preserve the power of men.

*nun = a member of a religious community of women

④ Check your understanding

🔊
54

- What behaviors against women might be considered justified in the name of a religion?
- Do different religions oppose the idea of strong women? If so, specify the religions.
- Who is responsible for the undervaluing of women?

2 Build your vocabulary

Table 1

🔊 55

☑	English	Japanese
1 ❑	be denied basic human needs	
❑	women are poorly valued	
❑	be forced into labor	
❑	early marriage	
❑	a cultural or religious justification	
❑	fundamental human rights	
2 ❑	oppress women	
❑	Christianity and Buddhism	
❑	no matter how inexperienced	
❑	unequal treatment of	

1) Translate the terms above from English to Japanese.

2) Memorize

① 🐴 with your F/P .

　　Winner : Translate the first phrase above into Japanese and say it out loud.

　　Loser : 🖾 and translate the phrase back into English.

② Do the same for the other phrases, checking the boxes ☑ as you go.

③ ●⇄●

3) Respond

① 🖾

② Your teacher will read out the words and phrases in Japanese, one by one. Work with the rest of the class to translate the Japanese phrases back into English.

3 Discuss Pair up with your D/P and discuss the questions below.

🔊 56

- Can cultures or religions justify practices that undervalue women?
- Can the values specific to a culture or religion be changed?

Wrap-up

How does gender equality benefit society?

- Pair up with your F/P and list the possible benefits below. Discuss the question.

　　○ Career-focused women　　　　　○ Home-focused men
　　　　■ spur innovation in industry　　　■ do more housework
　　　　■ ...　　　　　　　　　　　　　■ ...

The universal language of humor

Can-dos
◎面白い話で，聞き手をほっこりさせられる。
◎平易な英語で書かれたまとまった話を読んで，そのあらすじとオチを伝えられる。

Task 1　Collect funny stories

1 Read in silence

🔖 with your **S** **P** .

Winner : Read the passage *Part-time job* to yourself.

Loser :　Read *Restroom* to yourself.

Part-time job (passage for 🔖 winners)
57

　　My friend works part time at a grocery store. When he started working there, he didn't know the difference between a head of lettuce and a head of cabbage.

　　One day I asked him, "How can you tell them apart?"

　　"It's cabbage when it feels heavier in my hands," he said.

Kaoru

Restroom (passage for 🔖 losers)
58

　　The other day I was washing my hands in a restroom at my university. A friend of mine came through the door and went into one of the stalls*.

　　"Hello," he called out.

　　"Hello," I called back.

　　A moment later he emerged from the stall with his cellphone to his ear. He hadn't even noticed me. I was embarrassed.

Shun

*stall ＝トイレの個室

2 Retell

① 🖼

② Tell each other your stories by playing the parts of Kaoru and Shun (🔖 to decide who goes first).

③ Exchange comments after each story.

④ 📖 and confirm your stories.

Task 2 — More to come

1 Read in silence

🏃 with your F/P .

Winner: Read the passage *Smart cream* to yourself.

Loser: Read *Taiyaki* to yourself.

Smart cream (passage for 🏃 winners)

🔊 59

One day I was texting on my smartphone while eating an ice cream cone. I had the smartphone in my right hand and the ice cream in my left. A friend came up to me for a chat. After our chat, I returned to my smartphone and ice cream. I nibbled at* my smart phone and got ice cream all over my fingers.

Taiga

*nibble at = かじって食べる

Taiyaki (passage for 🏃 losers)

🔊 60

One day I came home from school very hungry, so I looked for something to eat. A Taiyaki cake was sitting on the kitchen table. I rushed over to the cake, removed it from its package, and took a big bite. The cake tasted strange. I checked the label on the Taiyaki package. The label said, "For Dogs." I gave the cake to my dog.

Keisuke

2 Retell

① 🗂

② Tell each other your stories by playing the parts of Taiga and Keisuke (🏃 to decide who goes first).

③ Exchange comments after each story.

④ 📖 and confirm your stories.

1　Read in silence

with your D P .

Winner : Read the passage *Chorus festival* to yourself.
Loser :　Read *Glasses* to yourself.

🔊 61

Chorus festival (passage for 🀄 winners)

　Back in junior high school we had a chorus festival. I was the best pianist in my class. The teacher asked me to play with the chorus for the event. We rehearsed the song every day, both before and after school. When the day finally came, our class was the seventh to take the stage. The audience stared up at us in silence, eager to hear us

©Tomacco/Shutterstock.com

perform. As I played the first few bars*, none of my classmates in the chorus sang along. I played a few bars more, but no one joined in.

　The teacher jumped out from backstage. "You're playing a different song," she whispered. The chorus festival became a solo piano concert.

Ryo

*play a few bars = 2,3 小節弾く

Glasses (passage for 🀄 losers)

🔊 62

　In my second year of high school I had a boyfriend named Daisuke. He used to wear a pair of nice black glasses. That autumn we went on a school field trip to Taiwan. One day on the trip, we got together with a group of local high school students to make friends. After the get-together, I wanted to walk back to the bus with Daisuke. When I spotted his black glasses, I ran up to him and grabbed his arm. The arm belonged to a Taiwanese boy wearing the same black glasses. We stared at each other, embarrassed. I felt that I had somehow betrayed Daisuke.

Shihoko

2　Retell

① 📖

② Tell each other your stories by playing the parts of Ryo and Shihoko (🀄 to decide who goes first).

③ Exchange comments after each story.

④ 📖 and confirm your stories.

Task 4 — What about you?

1 **Talk and write**

① Pick out a funny story from your life and prepare a 2-minute version of the story. You have 10 minutes to prepare. Take notes, if necessary.

② Pair up with your **S** **P** and tell each other your stories (✌ to decide who goes first).

③ Write a first draft of your funny story in 15 minutes.

Task 5 — Stand up and tell your story

1 **Talk**

① Stand up with the rest of the class and find a new partner (someone you haven't yet spoken to today).

② Tell each other your stories (✌ to decide who goes first). Try not to look at your draft while you talk.

③ Find a different partner and repeat step ②.

Wrap-up

Write up and speak up

① Write out your story on a fresh sheet of paper. (10 minutes)

② Volunteer to tell your story to the class.

③ Turn in your story before you leave the classroom.

1 Listen and Read

① 🎧 Listen and repeat.

② Read aloud Pair up with your F/P and take turns reading the text aloud, sentence by sentence.

🔊 63

Ryo and I got married about twenty years ago. Like many couples, we planned our wedding and honeymoon at the same time. I suggested that we go to Tahiti, a place I had always wanted to see. Ryo agreed instantly. We imagined the beautiful blue ocean, white sandy beaches, and stunning sunsets on the faraway island.

A few days after we made our plan, we went to a travel agent to make reservations. We purchased the last available tickets on a direct flight to Tahiti in late July, the peak travel season. The travel agent booked us a luxurious honeymoon suite in a floating hotel. We were thrilled.

But later that night, Ryo looked anxious over dinner.

"Is something bothering you?" I asked.

"I'm worried that the airplane will be crowded," Ryo explained. "What if we can't find any seats? Will we have to stand all the way to Tahiti?"

He thought that the airplane would have straps to hang onto, like a train. My young fiancé had never flown on an airplane.

Kay

③ Check your understanding Ask each other the following questions. 🔊 64

- Where did Ryo and Kay plan to go for their honeymoon?
- What kind of scene did they imagine when they thought of the South Pacific?
- Where did they purchase their airplane tickets?
- What worried Ryo when they were arranging the tickets?
- What is the punchline of this story?

2 What about you?

① Speak up Your teacher will ask the class the following question.

- What country would be perfect for a romantic vacation with a special friend?

② Talk

1) Pair up with your ^D_P and ask each other the same question.

2)

| Optional task 2 | Learn from storybooks |

1 Retell

① Pick out a storybook with pictures (a book of your own, a book from the library, a book the teacher has brought to class, etc.).

② Read it through and prepare to tell the story in your own words.

③ Pair up with your SP and tell each other your stories (to decide who goes first).

Chapter 12

Humanitarian aid:
Médecins Sans Frontières

Can-dos
⊙ MSF（国境なき医師団）の活動を通じて，人道支援の可能性と困難点を知る。
⊙ インタビューで話題を広げたり焦点化したりしながら，やりとりを維持・発展できる。

Task 1 What is *Médecins Sans Frontières* (MSF)?

1 Speak up

Your teacher will ask you the questions below.

- Have you ever heard of Médecins sans frontières (MSF)? If you have, tell your partner about MSF. If not, imagine what the organization is.
- Do you sometimes help others in need?
- ...

Optional task 1

1 Watch

Your teacher will introduce MSF International by showing a short movie (https://www. msf.org/).

Task 2 Do you have the right personality to work for MSF?

1 Interview

① Interview your SP to decide if your SP has the right personality to work for MSF.

② 🖊

    Winner: Interviewer.

    Loser :   Interviewee. Answer "yes" or "no" and explain why.

③ Start the interview. Check off the questions as you go (✓).

④ ●⇄●

Table 1 | Interview questions
🔊 66

Yes	No	Questions
❏	❏	Do you have any interest in developing countries?
❏	❏	Do you sometimes feel stressed in your school or family?
❏	❏	Would you like to travel somewhere far away?
❏	❏	Do you want to get to know people from other cultures?
❏	❏	Do you want to improve your English?
❏	❏	Do you have any special talents?
❏	❏	Would "*Médecins Sans Frontières*" look good on your CV* (curriculum vitae)?
❏	❏	Would you like to work for an international organization such as the UN or UNHCR**?
❏	❏	Do you thirst for adventure?

*CV= a short written document that lists your education and previous jobs
**UNHCR = United Nations Higher Commissioner for Refugees

2 Assess

Count your partner's "Yes" answers and check Table 2 to determine MSF's recommendation.

Table 2

Number of "Yes" answers	You ☑	Your partner ☑	MSF's recommendation for your partner
0-4	❏	❏	Enjoy a peaceful but ordinary life.
5-7	❏	❏	Enjoy a mostly peaceful life but be adventurous when you can.
8-9	❏	❏	Join MSF now!

3 Interview

① 🎴 with your F/P .

Winner: Interviewer (See Table 1).

Loser: Interviewee. Offer more than simple "yes" or "no" answers.

② Start the interview. Check off the questions as you go (✓).

③ ⬤⇄⬤

1   **Speak up**

🔊 67

- What do you see in the picture?
- What do you think happened to the building?

Photo 1   Bombed-out MSF hospital

MSF154407 © Victor J. Blue

2   **Listen and talk**

① 🖾 and 🎧 .

② 🖾 and pair up with your .

③ Take turns asking each other the questions below.
- When did the bombing take place?
- What did MSF call for?

④ 🖾 and 🎧 .

⑤ 🖾 and repeat step ③ .

3   **Read and check your understanding**

🔊 68

Sudden airstrikes on Saturday, October 3, 2011 destroyed an MSF hospital building and the lives of many people. Shortly after 2 a.m., US gunships* began bombarding the main hospital building, instantly killing patients in their beds. According to the final estimation, 42 people lost their lives and 37 were injured. Some of the victims were shot from the air as they ran out from the burning building. Throughout the hour of devastation, MSF repeatedly asked the US military command to stop their gunships from bombing.

Days later, the US military accepted responsibility for what it described as a mistaken attack. They claimed that the bombing had been requested by Afghan government forces who had come under fire from anti-government guerillas. The MSF president called for a thorough and transparent investigation into this accident.

*gunship: an armed helicopter

4 **Listen and talk** How important was the hospital?

① 🎧 Listen and Repeat

② Read aloud Pair up with your **S P** and take turns reading the text aloud, sentence by sentence.

🔊 **69**

The bombed hospital was opened by Médecins Sans Frontières (MSF) in the northern Afghan city of Kunduz in August 2011 to provide free, high-quality medical care to the victims of accidents and violence. Before the hospital opened, people with severe injuries in the region had no local access to essential medical care. The nearest adequate medical facilities, in Pakistan and the Afghan capital of Kabul, could only be reached by long hours of travel over dangerous roads. Once the hospital was opened, it saved the lives of many people. The hospital was the best-equipped medical facility of its type in all of northeastern Afghanistan. Tragically, the hospital was destroyed only four years after it opened.

③ Check your understanding Ask each other the questions below.

- Who ran the hospital?
- Why was the hospital opened?
- How did life change for the local community after the hospital was opened?

(**Task 4**) **How did MSF react?**

---

1 **Listen**

🎧 and 🎧 .

2 **Check your understanding**

🔊 **70**

 and pair up with your **F P** . Ask each other the questions below.

- Did the US president apologize to the MSF president over the phone?
- Did he use the word "sorry"?

(Photo 2) The MSF president

MSF166566/© Paulo Filgueiras

3 🎧 **Listen and dictate** Fill in the blanks as you listen again.

Interviewer : I suppose you spoke personally to the US president. Is that
(co   )?

Joanne : Indeed, I did.

Interviewer : What did he say to you?

Joanne : He apologized for the attack and accepted full (re   ). He is
fully committed to conducting a (tr   ), thorough
(in   ) into what happened.

Interviewer : Did he use the word "sorry"?

Joanne : I'm having trouble recalling. He spoke so quickly.

Interviewer : Did he sound (em   ) engaged and involved?

Joanne : That was hard to tell just from hearing his voice on the phone. I don't
often speak to presidents.

4 **Role play**

① 🗣 with your $\boxed{\frac{F}{P}}$.

    Winner : Read the part of the Interviewer aloud.

    Loser : Read Joanne's part aloud.

② Translate your parts aloud in Japanese.

③ Repeat your parts in English.

Task 5 **What did we learn from the accident?**

☐ **Share**

① Pair up with your $\boxed{\frac{D}{P}}$ and ask each other the question below.

    • What lessons can be learned from this accident?

② Share your views with the class.

Task 6 — What do we know about MSF?

1 Read in silence

[1] Principle and Financing:

Médecins Sans Frontières (MSF, or "Doctors without Borders" in English) is an independent medical humanitarian organization founded in 1971. Today the organization deploys some 35,000 people on the ground in roughly 70 countries. MSF provides lifesaving medical care to those affected by war, natural disasters, disease outbreaks, and other crises. MSF personnel work in accordance with international humanitarian law and medical ethics, treating people based on medical needs regardless of race, religion, or political affiliation. They are unique for their financial independence: almost 90% of MSF's funding comes from private donors, not governments. This reliance on private funding allows MSF to make rapid operational decisions based on medical needs, not on political considerations. MSF won the Nobel Peace Prize in 1999.

[2] Humanitarian aid:

Humanitarian aid (HA), a mission of MSF, is meant to help people in need. By definition, HA is administered to preserve and respect people's lives and restore their autonomy. These purposes set HA apart from developmental aid and encourage the participation of private and independent humanitarian organizations as key players. HA should be inherently impartial, and its actions should be useful to others and based on goodwill. While HA will always be subject to limitations and contradictions, it should uphold the ideal of solidarity between the peoples of the world without being swayed by political forces.

2 Check your understanding

① Pair up with your [F/P] and ask each other the questions below.

paragraph [1]

- What is MSF?
- When was MSF founded?
- What is MSF free from?
- From where does the MSF funding come?
- What award did MSF receive in 1999?

paragraph [2]

- Who does the MSF help and support?
- What is humanitarian aid intended to accomplish?
- What kinds of organizations play key roles in humanitarian aid?

② Speak up

Your teacher will ask several students to share their answers.

3 Build your vocabulary

Table 3

☑	English	Japanese
1 ☐	independent medical humanitarian organization	
☐	natural disaster	
☐	disease outbreak	
☐	financial independence	
☐	private donation	
☐	Nobel Peace Prize	
2 ☐	humanitarian aid	
☐	preserve and respect people's lives	
☐	restore their autonomy	

1) Translate the terms above from English to Japanese.

2) Memorize

① 🎴 with your [S][P].

Winner: Translate the first phrase above into Japanese and say it out aloud.

Loser: Close this book and translate the phrase back into English.

② Do the same for the other phrases, checking the boxes ☑ as you go.

③ [◉⇄◉]

3) Respond

①

② Your teacher will read out the words and phrases in Japanese, one by one. Work with the rest of the class to translate the Japanese phrases back into English.

| Task 7 | **Summarize MSF** |

1 **Speak up**

Your teacher will ask you the questions in Task 6 ② (p. 80) and write your answers on the board (Board 1).

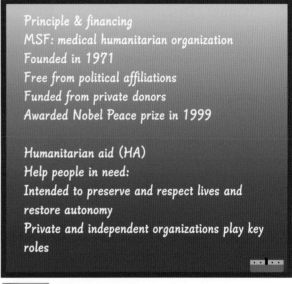

Principle & financing
MSF: medical humanitarian organization
Founded in 1971
Free from political affiliations
Funded from private donors
Awarded Nobel Peace prize in 1999

Humanitarian aid (HA)
Help people in need:
Intended to preserve and respect lives and restore autonomy
Private and independent organizations play key roles

Board 1 | Complete memo

2 **Explain**

① Your teacher will cross out some of the key words and phrases on the board (Board 2).

② Pair up with your S P and describe MSF together using the remaining keywords and phrases on the board.

③ Take turns making complete sentences with the keywords and phrases.

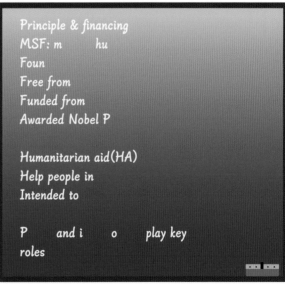

Principle & financing
MSF: m   hu
Foun
Free from
Funded from
Awarded Nobel P

Humanitarian aid(HA)
Help people in
Intended to

P   and i   o   play key roles

Board 2 | Half memo

3 Organize and memorize

① Your teacher will erase all of the key words and phrases, leaving only "Principle & Financing" and "Humanitarian Aid" on the board (Board 3).

②

Winner : Describe MSF.

Loser : Listen and add information, if necessary.

③ [icon]

④ [icon] and repeat steps ② and ③.

Board 3 Skeleton memo

4 Write [icon] and describe MSF.

MSF

Optional task 2 — Research

1 Talk

Pair up with your **S** **P** and ask each other the questions below.

🔊 **76**

- Do you know the man in Photo 3 ?
- Is he still alive?
- What country did he help?
- How did he contribute to the well-being of the people?
- What is his message for you personally?
- What is his message for the world?
- ...

2 Share

Research his story with your **S** **P** and share your findings with another pair.

Photo 3

© Peshawar-kai

Wrap-up

Share **What do you do to help people in need?**

① Pair up with your **D** **P** and ask each other, "What do you do to help people in need?"

② Stand up, walk around in the classroom, and find a partner you have not yet spoken to today. Ask each other the above question.

③ 🖼️

Chapter 13

Petite Debate:
Solo debate and personal topics

Can-dos
◎日常的な話題について，即興で理由と根拠を添えて 1 分間話すことができる。
◎日常的な話題について，100-150 語のまとまったエッセイを書くことができる。

Task 1 — Where are you going?

1 Speak up Your teacher will ask the class the questions below.

🔊 77

- Are you planning a trip somewhere in the coming holidays?
- Where will you go?
- Who will you go with?
- What do you want to do there?
- ...

2 Talk

Pair up with your S P and ask each other the same questions.

Task 2 — Traveling in Japan or traveling abroad?

1 Speak up

Your teacher will ask where you like traveling better, in Japan or abroad. Answer the question and give your reasons. The teacher will jot down your reasons next to your name on the board (Board 1).

Traveling in Japan is better than traveling abroad.	Traveling abroad is better than traveling in Japan.
Tatsuma: safe Yui: cheaper	Yuki: more exciting Kazuma: cultures

Board 1

2 Debate It's your turn

① 🏃 with your SP .

Winner : Choose your position.

Loser :　Take the other position.

② Follow the steps in Table 1 .

Table 1 Petite Debate Procedure

	Phase	Duration	Activity
1	Brainstorming	2 min.	Organize your argument. Take notes if necessary.
2	Stand up and 🏃		Decide who goes first.
3	Constructive arguments	2 min.	Present your arguments (1 min. for each side).
4	Sit down		

Language 1 State your conclusion first and present two good reasons to support it

① 🎧 **Listen and repeat**

② **Read aloud** Pair up with your SP and read the two arguments aloud to each other.

Table 2 Examples of arguments to support your opinion

78

Traveling in Japan	Traveling abroad
Hi, everyone. I strongly believe that traveling in Japan is better than traveling abroad. **I would like to offer two points. First**, Japan is safe. **Second**, Japan has hot springs. **Let me start with my first point, on the issue of** safety. Japan is said to be the safest country in the world. People are honest and calm, and gun ownership is strictly controlled. The Japanese police are also known for their high reliability. **My second point is about** hot springs. Hot springs seem to be everywhere in Japan, but overseas they are hard to find. Hot springs are refreshing and healthy …	**Hi guys. In my opinion**, traveling abroad is far superior to traveling in Japan. **I would like to offer two points to support this view**. **My first point relates to** culture. Overseas travel allows us to experience different cultures. By learning about customs and traditions in other countries, we gain insight into how we live here in Japan. **My second point relates to** international communications. When travelers go abroad, they can use the English they studied at school. As their English improves through practice, their skills in international communications will get better. …

Task 3 — Improve your argument

① Argue the same position you argued in [Task 2] [2] (p. 85).

② Follow the steps in [Table 1] (p. 85). Try to use the sentences and phrases in **bold font** in [Table 2] (p. 85).

Task 4 — DVDs vs. movie theaters

① 🖳 with your [F][P].

Winner: Choose your position.

Loser: Take the other position.

② Follow the steps in [Table 1]. Begin the debate.

③ Pair up with your [D][P] and follow the steps in [Table 1] (🖳 to decide your position).

Traveling in Japan is better than traveling abroad.	Traveling in Japan is better than traveling abroad.
Tatsuma: safe Yui: cheaper	Yuki: more exciting Kazuma: cultures
DVD	Movie theater

Board 2

Task 5 — More topics

Your teacher will write several new topics on the board, one by one ([Board 3]).

① Rotate seats to change partners ([Figure 1](p. 87)) and debate the next topic, "city life vs. rural life."

② 🖳 to decide your position and follow the steps in [Table 1]. Begin the debate.

③ Repeat steps ① and ② with different topics (*e.g.*, "single vs. married" or "traveling alone vs. traveling with someone").

Traveling in Japan is better than traveling abroad.	Traveling in Japan is better than traveling abroad.
Tatsuma: safe Yui: cheaper	Yuki: more exciting Kazuma: cultures
DVD city life single traveling alone	Movie theater rurla life married traveling with someone

Board 3

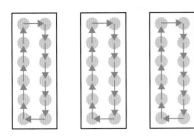

Board	

Figure 1 Rotate clockwise

Task 6) Choose your topics

① Rotate seats (Figure 1) to change partners.

② Choose a topic from Table 3 .

③ 📱 to decide your position

④ Follow the steps in Table 1 . Begin the debate.

⑤ Rotate seats and repeat steps ② to ④.

Table 3 List of topics

Which do you prefer?	
classroom classes	online classes
paying by credit card	paying by cash
reading books	watching movies
sports	art
high school	university
shopping around town	shopping online
The Olympics	world cup soccer
Japanese food	Italian food
Japanese inns or *ryokans*	hotels
e-books	paper books
rainy days	sunny days
spring	autumn
automobiles	bicycles
convenience stores	supermarkets
school in April	school in September

Wrap-up

Write an essay of 100 to 150 words on any topic that interests you. (15 minutes)

Topic

Chapter 14

Team debate: Go global

Can-dos
⊙ ペアで役割分担をして効果的な主張と反論ができる。
⊙ Global issue について 100-150 語のまとまったエッセイを書くことができる。

Task 1 — Debate with rebuttal

1 Speak up

① Team up with your $\frac{F}{P}$ and compete against your $\boxed{S}\boxed{P}$'s (team versus team).
② Your teacher will write out two opposing opinions (Board 1).
③ 🎲 to decide your position.
④ Follow the steps in Table 1 .

> *Traveling in Japan is better than traveling abroad.*
>
> *Traveling abroad is better than traveling in Japan.*

Board 1

Table 1 Team debate procedure

Phase	Duration	Activity
1. Brainstorming	2 min.	Decide who on your team argues FOR your team's opinion and who argues AGAINST the other team's opinion. Organize your arguments. Take notes if necessary.
2. 🎲		Decide which team speaks first.
3. FOR arguments	Each team speaks for 1 min.	Present your FOR arguments
4. AGAINST arguments	Each team speaks for 1 min.	Present your AGAINST arguments

| Team A FOR argument | Team B FOR argument | Team A AGAINST argument | Team B AGAINST argument |

Figure 1 Speaking order

① 🎧 **Listen and repeat**

② **Read aloud**

Read the arguments aloud by taking the part you took in ⟨Task 1⟩ ①.
Follow the speaking order in ⟨Figure 1⟩.

⟨Table 2⟩ FOR and AGAINST arguments

🔊 78

	Traveling in Japan	Traveling abroad
For	**Hi, everyone. I strongly believe** that traveling in Japan is better than traveling abroad. **I would like to offer two points. First,** Japan is safe. **Second,** Japan has hot springs. **Let me start with my first point, on the issue of** safety. Japan is said to be the safest country in the world. People are honest and calm, and gun ownership is strictly controlled. The Japanese police are also known for their high reliability. **My second point is about** hot springs. Hot springs seem to be everywhere in Japan, but overseas they are hard to find. Hot springs are refreshing and healthy.	**Hi guys! In my opinion,** traveling abroad is far superior to traveling in Japan. **I would like to offer two points to support this view.** **My first point relates to** culture. Overseas travel allows us to experience different cultures. By learning about people's customs and traditions in other countries, we gain insight into how we live here in Japan. **My second point relates to** international communications. When travelers go abroad, they can use the English they studied at school. As their English improves through practice, their skills in international communications get better.

Hot springs: *Nyuto-onsen* (Akita)

Against

Our opponents argue that traveling abroad is better because it offers the opportunity to experience different cultures and use English. **Their arguments no longer apply in the 21st century**. A person can now experience different cultures even within Japan. Many people visit Japan every year. They bring with them their own cultures from different parts of the world. Why should a Japanese person go to the trouble and expense of an overseas trip, when rich world cultures can be experienced at home? We in Japan can also use English by speaking with overseas visitors. We might want to tell them the way to a station, for example, or recommend what they should buy as a souvenir ...

Our opponents argue that traveling in Japan is better. **We strongly oppose their position**. Japan, they assert, is the safest country. **This is not the case**. Japan is often struck by natural disasters that endanger many thousands of lives. All of you surely remember the Great East Japan Earthquake (Higashi-nihon Daisinsai). Our opponents also tell us that Japan has hot springs. **Is this relevant?** If you were a tourist, would you bother to visit a hot spring? Taking a hotel room shower is so much easier and more convenient. Some visitors to Japan might also feel restricted by the many rules to be followed in a hot spring ...

2 Build your vocabulary

Table 3

80

✓	English	Japanese
❏	Their arguments no longer apply in the 21st century.	
❏	We strongly oppose their position.	
❏	This is not the case.	
❏	Is this relevant?	

1) Translate the sentences above from English to Japanese.

2) Memorize

　① Pair up with your [F/P] and 👥 .

　　Winner: Translate the first sentence above into Japanese and say it out loud.

　　Loser:　📖 and translate the sentence back into English.

　② Do the same for the other sentences, checking the boxes ☑ as you go.

　③ [●⇄●] .

3) Respond

　① 📖

　② Your teacher will read out the sentences in Japanese, one by one. Work with the rest of the class to translate the Japanese sentences back into English.

Task 2　Go global

① Keep the same partner and opponents in [Task 1].

② Topic disclosure
Your teacher will choose a new topic from [Table 4](p. 92) and write it out on the board ([Board 2]).

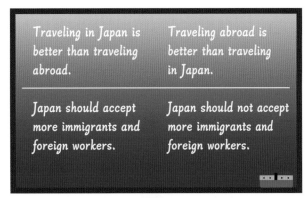

Traveling in Japan is better than traveling abroad.

Traveling abroad is better than traveling in Japan.

Japan should accept more immigrants and foreign workers.

Japan should not accept more immigrants and foreign workers.

Board 2

③ 🖐 to decide your opinion.

④ Debate your opinions by following the steps in [Table 1].

⑤ Change opponents
Use the seating rotation method to change opponents ([Figure 2]).

⑥ Repeat steps ② to ④.

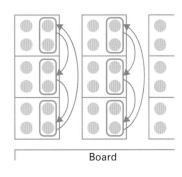

Board

Figure 2

Task 3　Choose new topics and debate

① Change opponents ([Figure 2]).

② Choose a new topic from [Table 4] and 🖐 to decide your opinion.

③ Follow the steps in [Table 1].

④ Repeat steps ① to ③. Enjoy the debate.

Table 4 | Debate topics

☑		
❏	The pandemic has damaged our lives terribly.	The pandemic has been a valuable learning opportunity for society.
❏	More and more people will travel abroad in the future.	Fewer and fewer people will travel abroad in the future.
❏	Working online is better than working at an office.	Working at an office is better than working online.
❏	China will overtake the US as a superpower sooner or later.	The US will remain the world's No. 1 superpower for the time being.
❏	Nuclear power plants should be shut down.	Nuclear power plants should keep running.
❏	The most massive, immediate problem in the world is poverty.	The most massive, immediate problem in the world is not poverty.
❏	All clothing should be unisex.	Clothing "for men" or "for women" is not outdated.
❏	Médecins Sans Frontières should rely on government support to carry out its mission.	Médecins Sans Frontières should not rely on government support to carry out its mission.
❏	Violating human rights for cultural or religious reasons is sometimes acceptable.	Human rights must never be violated, even for cultural or religious reasons.
❏	Gender equality is achievable.	Gender equality is not achievable.
❏	Japan should accept more immigrants and foreign workers.	Japan should not accept more immigrants and foreign workers.
❏	Free trade should take priority over the protection of domestic industries.	The protection of domestic industries should take priority over free trade.
❏	Technology leads to a better life	Technology does not lead to a better life.
❏	Automobiles are better than bicycles.	Bicycles are better than automobiles.
❏	Being happy is easier than it ever was before.	Being happy isn't getting easier in today's world.
❏	Same-sex marriage should be legal.	Same-sex marriage should not be legal.
❏	Married women should be able to keep their maiden names.	Married women should take their husbands' family names.
❏	The world is getting better.	The world is getting worse.
❏	...	...

Write an essay of 100 to 150 words on a topic that interests you.

Chapter 15

Another Story

Can-dos
◉今の自分に影響を与えた場所や時間を，将来の目標や Global issue と関連づけて印象的に表現できる。
◉協同して *Another Story* の実施と演出に貢献できる。

1 What is *Another Story*?

Another Story is a story about a special place where a person has changed or grown. Give a presentation on such a place in your own life. Try to relate your experience of that place to a global issue, if possible. The place might be:

- A town or country where you studied abroad
- A class or club in high school
- A tennis court, a convenience store, a mountaintop, or the sea
- Any place you have discovered something new

2 Prepare your *Another Story* presentation

- Make your presentation honest and impressive.
- Prepare your *Another Story* presentation **as homework**.
- Talk for around **3 minutes**.
- Use presentation software such as PowerPoint (PPT).
- Use text, video, music, photos, illustrations—whatever you like.

3 Presentation schedule

- Your teacher will tell the class when the presentations are to be given (Table 1), and in what order. You will have 1 or 2 weeks to prepare.

Table 1 *Another Story* Program (example)

Date	Order	Name	MC	Timekeeper	Helper with PC
◯◯	1	Natsu	Ryo	Daisuke	Shuhei
	2	Miku			
	3	Tensei			
	4	Noriko			
	...	...			
◯◯	11	Ryo	Miku	Noriko	Tensei
	12	Miho			
	13	Daisuke			
	14	Shuhei			
	...	...			

4 Example presentations

Your teacher will show two examples of *Another Story* presentations.

🔊 82

Example 1 Nanami found *Another Story* in the Philippines.

The Philippines

Last summer I visited the Philippines with a group of volunteers from my university. While working with the local children, we came to see the serious problems they faced in their lives.

Preparing dinner

Many of them were forced to drop out of school without good prospects for the future. Others were convinced that they had no pathway to success.

Queueing up to the camera

The children always managed to smile brightly, in spite of their hardships. Never have I seen children so cheerful in Japan.

Study work

I believe that their good spirits are rooted in the strong bonds between people in their community. When a person is in need, others reach out to help them. Being poor does not necessarily mean being unhappy.

The whole gang

When I think back to my visit to the Philippines, I wonder, "What does happiness mean for me?"

Nanami

Example 2 Shihoko found *Another Story* on the tennis court.

workplace

I found *Another Story* in the Ariake Tennis Forest. As a university freshman I joined a tennis club thinking it would be a lot of fun.

dismay

But the many hours of practice were tough-going and brought me no joy. Tennis seemed pointless. I began to think of quitting the club.

at work

One day, a club mate asked me to take a part-time job as a "ball person." The request changed my life. A ball person picks up balls on the court and supplies them to a tennis player competing in a match. Through my time as a ball person, I discovered a joy in tennis I would never otherwise have discovered.

limitless possibility

What moved me most was the players' concentration on every stroke, every ball, and every game. They devoted so much to the game. I decided that year to devote myself fully to everything I did. That's the game plan for the rest of my life.

Shihoko

Materials to prepare

Students

- Presentation data

Teacher

- A room with a PC and projector screen
- The program (Table 1 (p. 94))
- A remote controller, if available
- A beeper or bell, if available (a smartphone will work)

1 Before the presentation

Work together to make your *Another Story* presentations unforgettable.

1. **Setting**: Arrange the tables and chairs as shown in Figure 1 (the arrangement depends on the room layout and equipment).
2. **Roles**: Volunteer to take one of the roles below.
   - **MC**: Organizes the event and invites comments or questions after each presentation.
   - **Helper with the PC**: Help the presenters with the PC.
   - **Timekeeper**: Keeps time during the 3-minute presentation and uses a beeper to let the speaker know when 1-minute remains (at the 2-minute point) and when the presentation ends.

Figure 1

2 Begin the presentation

3. Welcome the first presenter and give a big hand of applause.
4. The next presenter takes a seat at the front of the class to save time.

Another Story presentation

3 After the presentation

5. Volunteer to ask questions or make comments.
6. The teacher will make concluding remarks.
7. Work together to reset the tables and chairs.

Key questions
to Global Issues

☑	Questions	chapter
❑	Have you ever been abroad?	1
❑	Do you think Japan should take a more active role in banning nuclear weapons?	2
❑	What's troubling you these days?	3
❑	What are you addicted to?	3
❑	Have you ever been unable to gain access to clean water, basic sanitation, or modern health services?	4
❑	Can you do anything to help solve environmental problems?	4
❑	Tell us about a global issue that interests you.	5
❑	What was Ms. Ogata Sadako's message for the world/Japan?	6
❑	Would someone miss your skills and expertise if you emigrated to another country?	6
❑	When you see a foreign part-time worker in a convenience store, construction site, or somewhere else in Japan, do you start up a chat?	7
❑	Should Japan accept more immigrants and refugees?	7
❑	Do you think that immigrants fill useful jobs in Japan's workforce?	7
❑	How can Japan welcome immigrants to help them live comfortably and contribute to Japanese society?	7
❑	What lesson did you learn from the Barumbans?	8
❑	Shouldn't high school students be allowed to dye their hair?	9
❑	Do you think that people with disabilities contribute less to society than people without disabilities?	9
❑	Why do you think Japanese women are falling behind in the attainment of professional qualifications?	10
❑	Do you think gender equality is advancing around the world/in Japan?	10
❑	Can cultures or religions justify practices that undervalue women?	10
❑	Can the values specific to a culture or religion be changed?	10
❑	How does gender equality benefit society?	10

❏	Pick out a funny story from your life and prepare a 2-minute version of the story.	11
❏	Do you sometimes help others in need?	12
❏	What is humanitarian aid intended to accomplish?	12
❏	What is Mr. Nakamura Tetsu's message for you personally?	12
❏	Which one do you like better, traveling alone or traveling with someone?	13
❏	Do you think that the world is getting better or worse?	14
❏	Tell us your *Another Story*.	15

著者紹介

柳川浩三（やながわ　こうぞう）法政大学准教授

小田原に育ち，25年間の神奈川県立高校教師を経て現職。

「学生が選ぶベストティーチャー賞：グローバル・語学部門」受賞（法政大学主催2019年度）。

研究し，実践する英語教師を目指して五里霧中（夢中）。

Simon Johnson（サイモン・ジョンソン）フリーランス・ライター

米国カリフォルニア州ロサンゼルス出身。多国籍企業（三菱商事, 凸版印刷）, JICA, 官民団体
向け英文出版物の作成に長年携わる。

執筆協力

甲斐　順

白井龍馬

須永美奈子

鈴木脩馬

タスクで考える国際問題

自分の中のテクストを探して

2021年3月30日　第1版発行
2023年9月30日　第3版発行

著　　者──柳川浩三　Simon Johnson

発 行 者──前田俊秀

発 行 所──株式会社三修社

〒150-0001 東京都渋谷区神宮前2-2-22
TEL. 03-3405-4511 / FAX. 03-3405-4522
振替 00190-9-72758
https://www.sanshusha.co.jp
編集担当　松居奈都

印刷・製本──日経印刷株式会社

表紙デザイン ──────土橋公政
本文デザイン・DTP──川原田良一
本文図版・イラスト ─── 久保理沙子
準拠音声録音・制作──高速録音株式会社

教科書準拠CD発売

本書の準拠CDをご希望の方は弊社までお問い合わせください。